GRADE VOCABULARY

Fun-filled Activities

Om KIDZ

An imprint of Om Books International

Alphabetical Order

Alphabetical order is a way to sort a list. It is done by following the usual order of letters in an **alphabet**.

> **bus, engine, airplane, helicopter, car**
>
> ↓
>
> **airplane, bus, car, engine, helicopter**

Alphabetical order makes it easier to find a name or a title in the list.

Rewrite each word list in ABC order

hop, top, pop, mop

grass, flower, bench, tree

shoes, jacket, trousers, cap

cupcake, pastry, bread

1. _____

2. _____

3. _____

4. _____

Alphabetical Order

Find the words in the word search below. Then write the words in the alphabetical order.

B	I	R	T	H	D	A	Y	
J	O	L	G	I	F	T	S	
F	R	O	S	T	I	N	G	
K	T	L	H	A	P	P	Y	
L	H	L	O	C	A	K	E	
M	W	I	S	H	R	O	A	
N	J	P	E	I	T	K	A	
O	M	O	F	D	Y	R	V	
P	I	P	C	F	E	W	D	
I	C	E	C	R	E	A	M	

happy birthday wish ice cream cake gifts frosting lollipops party

1. _____ 2. _____ 3. _____

4. _____ 5. _____ 6. _____

7. _____ 8. _____ 9. _____

Sorting Words

Write the words under the right categories.

Food	Drink

pasta	milk	eggs	tea	cornflakes
patty	coffee	cheese	water	toast
noodles	almonds	butter	kiwi	bread

 TRY IT! In which list will you add ice?

Sort the Words into Different Categories

Read the words and sort them according to their categories. Write them under the right categories.

eyebrows, short, market, shoes, tall, grandmother, nose, bank, zoo, jacket, cheeks, long, airport, big, lips, aunt, gloves, daughter, trousers, mother

Women in the family	Places	Things you wear	Parts of your face	Size words

 TRY IT! Add one word of your choice each to the list on this page.

Words That Go Together

In each tile, colour three words that go together. Find the words across, down and even diagonally.

book	rain	light
cars	magazine	sun
clock	chair	newspaper

bird	goat	squirrel
grass	ladybug	orange
pillow	quilt	blanket

vast	sick	squid
huge	happy	octopus
giant	healthy	drawers

drill	grandma	cucumber
square	eggplant	sea
spinach	wise	sleep

woods	cookies	twelve
sky	mountain	forest
sausage	tomato	trousers

lake	pond	stream
indigo	pink	poppy
bark	branch	nest

Odd One Out

In each group, find the word that is not like the others. Circle it.

1. pills, doctor, hospital, secretary, nurse

2. aunt, sister, mother, uncle, niece

3. shoe, skirt, shirt, suit, smart

4. Thursday, November, December, May, April

5. good, nice, friendly, kind, tawny

6. beak, wings, ducklings, claws, feathers

Words with Related Meanings

Put a (✔) on the correct word.

1. Which two words name things you drink from?

   glass   cup   plate

2. Which two words name things you do with your eyes?

   watch   see   tell

3. Which two words name things you do with money?

   pay   sell   buy

4. Which two words name ways to make art?

   draw   paint   cut

5. Which two words tell you that something is not old?

   young   ancient   new

6. Which two words tell you how sure you are?

   know   guess   sure

7. Which two words name bad feelings?

   cross   jolly   angry

Difference Between Related Words

Circle the correct option for each question below.

1. Which one of these is inside?

   the ground   the floor

2. Which belongs to you?

   a pet   an animal

3. Which is faster?

   stroll   run

4. Which of these is younger?

   calf   cow

5. Which is bigger?

   a jump   a leap

6. Which is more sudden?

   pulling   yanking

7. Which is stronger?

   a wind   a breeze

8. Which is later?

   in the evening   at night

Synonyms

A synonym is a word that has nearly the same meaning as another word.
For example: tiny-wee

Match the words to their synonyms.

1. cry   hot

2. silent   hard

3. warm   fast

4. far   weep

5. difficult   correct

6. start   wealthy

7. alone   quiet

8. true   begin

9. quick   lonely

10. rich   distant

Synonyms

Choose the correct word and write the synonym for the words given below.

large   yell   noisy   sugary   gift   talk

speak _____

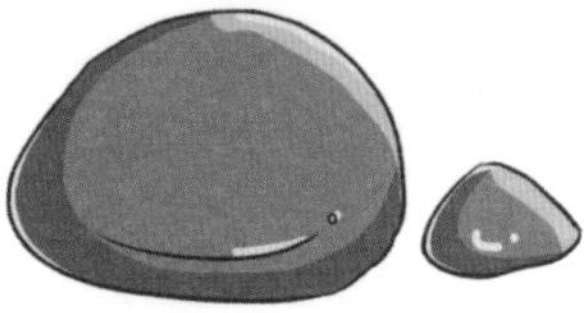

big _____

present _____

shout _____

loud _____

sweet _____

Synonyms

Using the across and down clues, write the matching words in the crossword below.

<table>
<tr><td>Across</td></tr>
</table>

Across

4. commented   8. rock
5. loaf   9. shortly

Down

1 task   6 grade
2 donate   7 rush
3 record   8 stain

a. list   b. chores   c. rank   d. give   e. spot
f. bread   g. stone   h. soon   i. dash   j. said

Antonyms

An antonym is a word that is opposite in meaning to another word.
For example: new-old

Choose the word that has the opposite meaning of the first word in each set.

1. quiet   noisy   silent

2. tidiness   clean   mess

3. loose   tight   fixed

4. shallow   wet   deep

5. deny   take   accept

6. none   every   zero

7. shrink   narrow   grow

8. polite   rude   generous

 TRY IT! Write as many antonyms as you can for the word, big. How many did you find?

Antonyms

Choose the best antonym for the following words and show Kate the way to reach the cottage and hide.

break
seek
weak
win
remove
leave
exit

Hide
_____

Reach
_____

Enter
_____

Strong
_____

Lose
_____

Repair
_____

Add
_____

Antonyms

foolish	difficult
sour	lost
never	new
disagreed	dislike
common	found

Write the antonym of the underlined words.

1. I have <u>found</u> my favourite toy.

   _____

2. The test was <u>easy</u> for me.

   _____

3. Jane <u>always</u> does her work on time.

   _____

4. Mother <u>likes</u> some hot water with lemon.

   _____

5. Roger's team <u>won</u> the soccer match.

   _____

6. The farmer picked some <u>sweet</u> apples
   from the orchard.

   _____

7. We all <u>agreed</u> with our new captain.

   _____

8. The teacher showed us picture of
   <u>rare</u> animals.

   _____

9. Eddie was <u>wise</u> to jump into the cool pool.

   _____

10. Let us decorate the class with <u>old</u> ribbons.

   _____

Compound Word

A compound word is a new word formed by putting two words together.

For example: back + pack = backpack

Circle the two words each compound word is made of.

newspaper   lunchbox

airplane   pancake

blueberry   bathrobe

pancake   armchair

thunderstorm   watermelon

Add a word to each of these words below to make a compound word of your own.

1. cow + _____ = _____

2. honey + _____ = _____

3. pen + _____ = _____

4. sea + _____ = _____

5. sun + _____ = _____

Compound Word

Make compound words. Number the puzzle pieces on the right to match the pieces on the left.

Compound Word

Complete the compound words in each sentence.

1. We use a _____ **pick** to pick at food stuck in a tooth.

2. I made a new _____ **house** for my dog.

3. Aunt Polly is making _____ **cakes** for us.

4. I saw a _____ **boy** ride the horse home.

5. The heavy rain _____ **thing** wet.

6. The dog chased the cat to the _____ **yard**.

7. Kate has a healthy _____ **fast** every morning.

8. My little brother likes to play in the _____ **box**.

9. The baker dressed the pizza with ham and _____ **apple**.

10. Drop the letters in the _____ **box**.

Prefix and Suffix

Prefix

A prefix is a word part placed at the beginning of a word. It changes the meaning of a word.

Read the common prefixes, their meanings and words as examples.

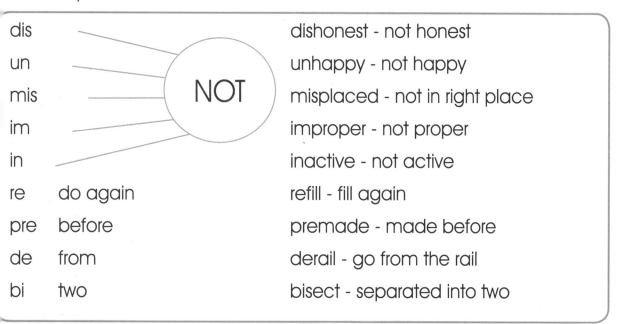

dis		dishonest - not honest
un		unhappy - not happy
mis	NOT	misplaced - not in right place
im		improper - not proper
in		inactive - not active
re	do again	refill - fill again
pre	before	premade - made before
de	from	derail - go from the rail
bi	two	bisect - separated into two

Prefixes

Choose and add a suitable prefix to the given words to make new words.

_____ stop

_____ fund   _____ test

_____ fair   _____ behave

_____ like   _____ real

_____ play   _____ turn

Dis
Non
Re
Un
Pre
Mis
Bi

Prefixes

Add one of the prefixes to the words and complete the sentences.

un	re	pre	mis	dis

1. Grandma told me to wait till my birthday to _____ **wrap** the gifts.

2. The baker had to _____ **heat** the oven before he could put the cookies in.

3. Linda forgot her backpack and had to _____ **turn** home to get it.

4. Ashley was sad because she was _____ **able** to get tickets for the magic show.

5. I was about to fall as my shoelaces were _____ **tied**.

6. Imme had to _____ **do** the math problems.

7. Be careful not to _____ **spell** the words on the poster.

8. Sharon was being _____ **honest** when she did not tell the truth.

Suffixes

A suffix is a word part placed at the end of a word. It changes the meaning of a word.

Here are some common suffixes, their meaning and an example.

Suffix	Meaning	Example
-ful	full of	hopeful
-ist	person who is	artist
-ly	in a way	slowly
-ion	act of/ condition of being	protection
-less	without	helpless
-ible	can be	collectible
-ness	being	sickness
-able	can be	washable
-er/-or	one who	trainer/protector
-ish	having the quality of	childish
-dom	place or state of being	freedom

More Suffixes

Pick and add a suffix to each root word to make new words.

1. most   – _____
2. beauty   – _____
3. tour   – _____
4. cold   – _____
5. move   – _____
6. late   – _____
7. drive   – _____

**-ful
-ist
-ly
-ment
-er
-est
-able**

Circle the word that contains a suffix in each sentence below.

1. The team was hopeful to win the match.

2. The students of our class have a lot of unity.

3. Sam was very careless when running in the rain.

4. If you don't eat proper food, it will cause weakness.

5. Please don't throw that bag. It can be useful.

6. Mom bought a new gift for me that is portable.

7. The sunrise we saw over the mountains was really beautiful.

8. The warmest time of the year is best for growing these plants.

9. Many plants become droopy if you don't water them well.

10. The old man had a lot of wisdom.

Squirrels Serving

Use a prefix or suffix from the list to form a word for each meaning. Write each word in the puzzle.

1. write again

2. read wrongly

3. without care

4. able to agree

5. being kind

6. opposite of appear

7. use wrongly

8. not covered

9. state of being sick

10. opposite of honest

11. not fair

12. full of help

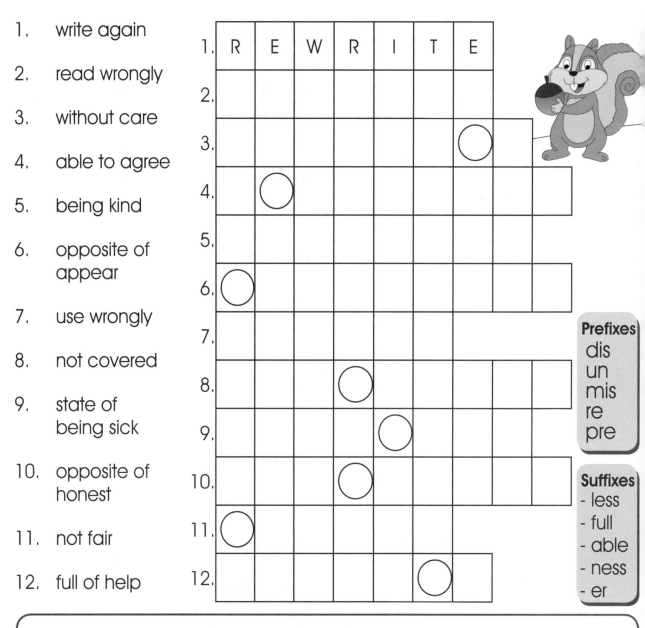

Prefixes
dis
un
mis
re
pre

Suffixes
- less
- full
- able
- ness
- er

What is a squirrel's favourite food? To solve the riddle, write each circled letter from above on the matching number below.

7   11   18   5   15   12   17   1   3

Homophones

SAME sounds

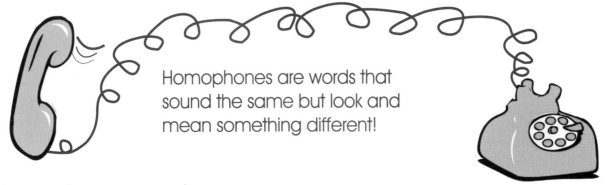

Homophones are words that sound the same but look and mean something different!

Let us read some examples.

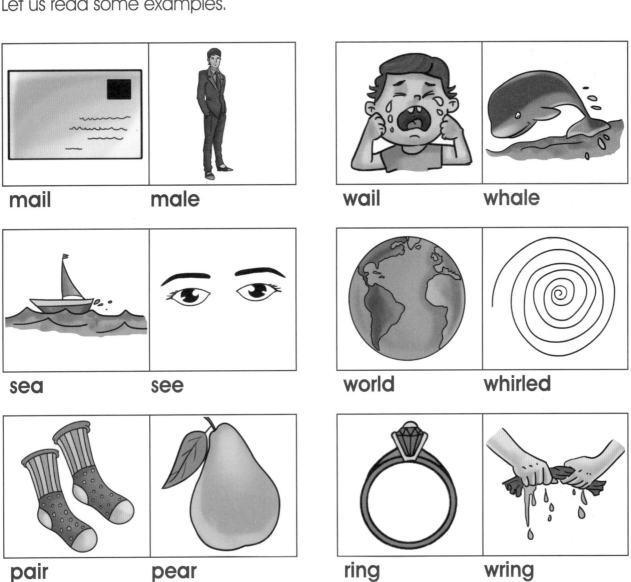

mail   **male**   **wail**   **whale**

sea   **see**   **world**   **whirled**

pair   **pear**   **ring**   **wring**

Drawing Homophones

Look at the picture and write a word for it. Now write its homophone and draw its picture.

	Right	
	_____	
	_____	
	_____	
	_____	

Writing Homophones

Write a homophone for each word given below.

1. be   –   _____

2. break   –   _____

3. i   –   _____

4. knot   –   _____

5. main   –   _____

6. ate   –   _____

7. dew   –   _____

8. no   –   _____

9. blew   –   _____

10. hair   –   _____

11. week   –   _____

12. some   –   _____

13. roll   –   _____

14. pain   –   _____

15. right   –   _____

 TRY IT! Think of two homophones of the word sent. Then write sentences to show the difference between the three words.

Writing Correct Homophones ◾

Choose the correct word to complete the sentence.

1. Last Monday, I _____ (road, rode) a pony along the trail in the mountains.

2. My dog hurt its _____ (paws, pause) from digging in the yard.

3. My sister _____ (passed, past) her time by reading stories.

4. My father cut the _____ (bored, board) in half to build a tree house.

5. We _____ (one, won) all the matches this year.

Make sentences with these pairs of homophones.

1. scene - seen

_____

_____

2. tail - tale

_____

_____

3. stair - stare

_____

_____

Homographs

Homographs are words that share the same spelling, regardless of how they are pronounced. Let us read some homographs.

bat

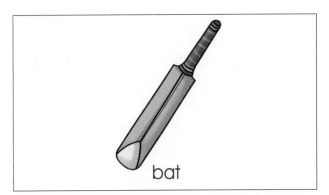

bat

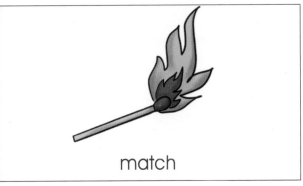

match

match

bank

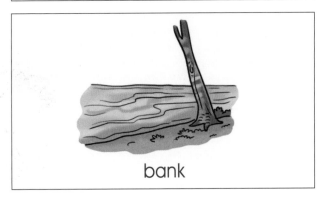

bank

bow

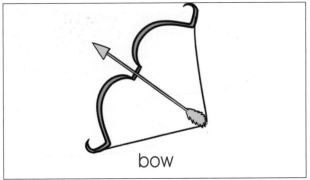

bow

Homographs

Use each word given below in sentences to show two different meanings it has. One has been done for you.

1. park - Dad parks his car in the garage.
    The children are playing in the park.

2. saw - _____

    _____

3. tie - _____

    _____

4. watch - _____

    _____

5. row - _____

    _____

GRAMMAR 1

The Sentence

A sentence is a group of words that is complete in itself. A sentence starts with a capital letter and ends with an end mark.

The dog is sleeping.

A sentence

A beautiful bird

not a sentence

Read the groups of words given below. Write S if it is a sentence and N if it is not a sentence.

1. We went to the park.

2. On the swings

3. The boys went on swings for an hour.

4. The bird and nest

5. The girls are skipping.

6. In the winter

7. The cat watched the bird on the tree.

8. All of us had fun at the park.

Try it! Write a sentence about yourself.

_____

Parts of a Sentence

A sentence has two parts – naming part and telling part.

Naming part of a sentence

<u>Bobby</u> rode on the merry-go-round.

naming part

<u>The merry-go-round</u> is high.

naming part

A naming part tells us who or what the sentence is about.

Bobby is the naming part.

The merry-go-round tells what this sentence is about.

QUICK CHECK
The naming part can be a **person**, **place**, **animal**, or **thing**.

Circle the naming part of these sentences.

1. Father and Carl went to the pool.
2. The day was hot.
3. The water was cold to touch.
4. Carl jumped into the pool with his father.
5. He took a tube to swim.
6. Carl liked to be in the cool water.
7. Father had fun in swimming too.

Try it!

Write a naming part for this sentence.

_____ went for a ride.

Parts of a Sentence

Telling part of a sentence.

Bobby <u>rode on the merry-go-round</u>.
       telling part

The merry-go-round <u>is high</u>.
                    telling part

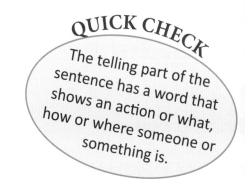

QUICK CHECK
The telling part of the sentence has a word that shows an action or what, how or where someone or something is.

A telling part tells us what someone or something does. It also tells us what/how someone or something is.

rode on the merry-go-round tells what Bobby did.

is high tells where the merry-go-round is.

Underline the telling part of these sentences.

1. Mary and Joy help mom in the kitchen.
2. Mother makes rice and fish for supper.
3. Joy wipes the plates.
4. Mary lays the table for supper.
5. Mother, Mary and Joy are happy.
6. They like to work together.

Try it!

Write a telling part for this sentence.
Kate and Jim _____

Put the Words in Order!

Which of these sentences uses the correct order of words? Tick the right answer.

1. I like eat to oranges.
2. Kim went to bed at 9.
3. Linda plays dolls with her.
4. Sail boat across the river.

Can you put the words in the correct order to form meaningful sentences? Write down the sentences in the correct word order.

1. Lia a dog pet has

_____

2. dog her pug is a named Tuff

_____

3. one year old is Tuff only

_____

4. has it brown a coat soft

_____

5. fond of eating it bread and milk is

_____

6. made a kennel Lia has Tuff for

_____

7. takes walk Lia her dog for evening in the a

_____

8. care takes Lia of Tuff good

_____

QUICK CHECK

Don't forget to begin the sentence with a capital letter and end with an end mark.

Try it! Use the word 'kennel' to make a sentence.

_____

Statements

A statement is a sentence that tells us something. A statement begins with a capital letter and ends with a period (.)

Neo likes to fly kites.
The kite is red and blue.

These sentences have capital letters and full stop placed incorrectly. Can you rewrite these statements correctly?

1. many people like to Fly. kites

   _____

2. kites Are made of. Paper

   _____

3. a kite is shaped. like a Diamond

   _____

4. nick likes to fly kites Too.

   _____

5. he has Made a kite. Shaped like a bird

   _____

6. it is. Fun to fly kites

   _____

Try it!

What kind of a kite would you like to fly? Write a statement about it.

_____

_____

Questions

A question is a sentence that asks for some information. A question begins with a capital letter and ends with a question mark (?)

Where are my books?
Have you seen my bag?

QUICK CHECK
Questions often begin with **who, what, when, where, why, how, do, did, will, can, is, am, are, was and were,** and so on.

Three of these sentences have full stops (.) in place of question mark (?). Identify and rewrite them using a question mark.

1. Mary and her family went to the zoo.

   _____

2. How far is the zoo.

   _____

3. They reached there in two hours.

   _____

4. Which animals did Mary see in the zoo.

   _____

5. Did they see the white tiger.

   _____

6. They had fun at the zoo.

   _____

Try it!

Write a question that you would ask Mary about her visit to the zoo.

_____

_____

Statements and Questions

Statement
- I like to play football.
- The bird is on the tree.

Question
- Which is your favourite game?
- Where is the bird?

Read each sentence below. Write 'St' for statement and 'Q' for question.

1. It is Tim's birthday today. ☐

2. How old is Tim? ☐

3. All his friends have come to wish him. ☐

4. The children are dressed in nice clothes. ☐

5. At what time will the party begin? ☐

6. I can see the beautifully decorated cake with pink and white icing. ☐

7. When will Tim cut the cake? ☐

8. There are many chairs in a row. ☐

9. Will the children play Musical Chairs? ☐

10. It will be fun at the party. ☐

Try it!

Put a full stop (.) at the end of the statement and a question mark (?) at the end of the question.
1. Where is James going with his sister
2. I am going to the beach

Exclamations

An exclamatory sentence expresses feelings. It shows excitement or surprise. Such sentences begin with a capital letter and end with an exclamation mark (!).
The garden is so beautiful!
Such pretty flowers it has!

Can you identify exclamations from the statements below? Put exclamation marks (!) for exclamatory sentences and full stops (.) for statements.

1. Jim and Tim went to the Shoe House ———

2. The Shoe House was so big ———

3. The boys ran inside the house ———

4. Oh, it was beautiful ———

5. Jim and Tim were happy ———

6. They played in the Shoe House ———

7. It was awesome ———

Try it!

Your mother bought a toy for you. Write an exclamatory sentence to express your answer.

_____

Commands

A command is a sentence that tells you to do something. A command begins with a capital letter. It ends with a period (.).

<u>D</u>on't shut the door<u>.</u>

<u>O</u>pen the windows<u>.</u>

QUICK CHECK

Statements usually begin with a noun or pronoun. Commands usually begin with a verb.

Tia is making fruit cream. Grandfather is telling Tia what to do. Rearrange the words and write each command correctly.

1. apples, and strawberries, cherries pomegranate pick up

   _____

2. all the wash fruits.

   _____

3. and remove cut cherries into half its pit.

   _____

4. pomegranate peel the.

   _____

5. and apples into chop strawberries small pieces.

   _____

6. sugar in put cream and a bowl and mix it.

   _____

7. all and mix the now add fruits well.

   _____

Try it! Think of one command your mother gave you. Write it down.

_____

Putting it Together!

Complete the sentences using words from the box. Then, write 'St' for statements, 'Q' for questions, 'E' for exclamations and 'C' for commands.

in the bushes	there	ball	puppy in his hands
move	the garden	the mud	ball in his hand

1. Amy looked around _____ □

2. Was someone hiding _____ □

3. Amy had a _____ □

4. Oh, he dropped the _____ □

5. He bent to _____ □

6. There were footprints on _____ □

7. Who was _____ □

8. Don't _____ □

9. Oh, it was a _____ □

10. Amy lifted the _____ □

QUICK CHECK

Don't forget to use:
- Period (.) at the end of a statement and command.
- Question mark (?) at the end of a question.
- Exclamation mark (!) at the end of an exclamatory sentence.

Naming Words or Nouns

A noun is a word that names a person, place, animal or thing.

Pam goes to the park.

The word 'Pam' names a person.

The word 'park' names a place.

Pam has a puppy.

The word 'puppy' names an animal.

Take the puppy on the bicycle.

The word 'bicycle' names a thing.

Here is a list of words. Select and separate these words into the different categories of nouns as given in the table.

| book | lion | Jim | doctor | dog | hen | Kate | school |
| pen | comb | house | pool | fish | Sim | mall | chair |

Person	Place	Animal	Thing

Try it! Write the names of a person, place, animal and thing that begin with the letter "R".

_____

To the Camp!

Pat went camping. Read the text below and circle the nouns.

QUICK CHECK
Do you remember that nouns name a person, place, animal or thing? Nouns are also names of insects, things in the sky and also words like **camp** and **hills**.

Pat and Neo went on a camping trip. The boys packed their bags. They packed shirts, shorts, socks and shoes. Neo took his hat. Pat took his books and toys. They went to the hills. The Sun was shining, the birds were singing, and the bees were buzzing. There were sheep too. Many boys and girls were on the camp. Both the boys went on a boat. It was fun at the camp.

Try it!

Write name of one person, place, animal and thing that you saw on your way to school yesterday.

_____

_____

_____

One and More than One

Nouns can name one or more than one.

A monkey is jumping on the tree.
The noun **monkey** names one.

The birds flew away from the tree.
The noun **birds** names more than one.
Many nouns that name more than one usually end with **s**.

Write the correct noun and complete the sentence.

1. A _____ and two birds were good friends.
   (tortoise/tortoises)

2. They lived on the banks of a _____ in
   a forest. (river/rivers)

3. The birds went to many _____.
   (place/places)

4. The tortoise felt sad that he could not
   go with them. He did not
   have _____. (wing/wings)

5. He told the birds to hold each end
   of a long _____ with their
   _____. (stick/sticks, beak/beaks)

6. He will hold the middle part
   of the stick with his _____.
   (mouth/mouths)

7. So he can fly with the _____ too!
   (bird/birds)

Try it! Write names of parts of your body that are more than one.
_____

Nouns Ending with -es

Many nouns that end with **s, sh, ch** and **x** add **-es** to name more than one.

bench- benches   box- boxes

dish- dishes   glass- glasses

Fill in the word grid by making these nouns more than one.

fox	dress	brush	bus	peach	watch	bush	sandwich

	b			h								
									f			
				w								b
		p	e		c							r
			t									
						d	r					
	b											
			s			w					s

Try it!

Correct the sentence.

The boxs are in the coachs.

_____

Nouns Ending with -ies

Some nouns end with **y** and have a consonant before it. Such nouns name more than one by removing **y** and adding **–ies**.

puppy- puppies
lady- ladies

Some nouns end in **y** and have a vowel before it. Such nouns name more than one just by adding **s**.
boy- boys
key- keys

Write the word that names more than one for each noun below.

1. monkey - _____
2. toy   - _____
3. baby   - _____
4. cherry   - _____
5. story   - _____
6. day   - _____
7. berry   - _____
8. tray   - _____
9. city   - _____
10. way   - _____

QUICK CHECK

a, e, i, o, u are vowels.
b, c, d, f, g, h, j, k, l, m, n, p, q, r, s, t, v, w, x, y, z are consonants.
For nouns that end with **y**, check whether **y** has a vowel or a consonant before it... to name it as more than one

Try it!

How will you write the word fairy to name more than one?

_____

Nouns Ending with -ves

Some nouns end with **f** or **fe**. Such nouns name more than one by removing **f** or **fe** and adding **–ves**.

loaf- loa<u>ves</u>

knife- kni<u>ves</u>

Circle the correct word that names more than one of the words given below.

1. calf – calfs calves
2. elf – elves elfs
3. half – halfs halves
4. chef – chefs cheves
5. wolf – wolves wolfs
6. life – lifes lives
7. giraffe – giraves giraffes
8. leaf – leaves leafs
9. cliff – cliffs clives
10. self – selves selfs
11. shelf – shelfs shelves
12. roof – roves roofs
13. thief – thiefs thieves
14. wife – wives wifes
15. chief – chiefs chieves

QUICK CHECK

Not all words ending in <u>f</u> or <u>fe</u> add - <u>ves</u> to them after removing <u>f</u> or <u>fe</u>. Some words just add <u>–s</u> to the words that end in <u>f</u> or <u>fe</u>

<u>Chefs</u>, <u>giraffes</u>, <u>roofs</u>, <u>chiefs</u>, <u>cliffs</u>

Try it!

How will you write the word 'scarf' to show more than one?

_____

Nouns Written Differently

Some nouns are written differently to denote more than one.

man – men   ox – oxen

child – children   foot – feet

Some nouns do not change to denote more than one.
one fish – many fish
one sheep – three sheep

Change these words to name more than one.

1. woman – women

2. mouse – _____

3. fish   – _____

4. goose – _____

5. child   – _____

6. ox   – _____

7. sheep – _____

8. deer   – _____

9. dice   – _____

10. tooth – _____

Try it! | Can you name the picture? What would you write for more than one of it?

 _____   _____

A or An

'A' and 'An' are articles. We use 'a' or 'an' before nouns that denote <u>one</u>.

'A' is used with noun words that begin with a <u>consonant</u>.

A bird sat on <u>a</u> rock.

'An' is used with noun words that begin with a <u>vowel</u> or <u>vowel sound</u>.

An emu laid <u>an</u> egg

Tick <u>a</u> or <u>an</u> for these words.

1. (a/an) apple and (a/an) pineapple

2. (a/an) monkey and (a/an) elephant

3. (a/an) banana and (a/an) orange

4. (a/an) ostrich and (a/an) owl

QUICK CHECK

Before writing a/an check if the word begins with a consonant or vowel/vowel sound. Do you remember the vowels and consonants?

Write <u>a</u> or <u>an</u> in the blanks and complete the text.

1. One day I saw _____ cat.

2. The cat was sitting on _____ fence under _____ umbrella.

3. The cat was having _____ ice cream.

4. _____ mouse came running near the cat.

5. It had _____ box.

6. There was _____ pen, _____ fork, _____ ink pot, _____ watch and _____ bat in the bag.

7. The mouse ran into _____ hole.

Try it! | Write names of 3 things you have in your school bag using a or an.
_____

Some Special Nouns

Special names of people, animals and places are called proper nouns. We begin all proper nouns with a capital letter.

Sim is my friend.

He has a pet cat. His cat's name is Kitty.

Sim and Kitty are proper nouns.

Underline the proper nouns in the paragraph given below. Are they written correctly? Mark each letter that should be in capital and rewrite the letter.

J
james is popo's friend. He went to meet his friend, popo yesterday.
=
He took his pet squirrel jojo with him. There he met uncle tim and aunt mary.
popo has a pet duck. He calls it doyo. popo gave jojo a few nuts
to eat. jojo enjoyed eating them. Soon joy, kate, neo and linda
came there. They all made a duck house for doyo.

Try it! Imagine you have a pet. What name would you like to give it? Now, write a sentence about your imaginary pet.

_____

Special Names of Places

Proper nouns are also special names of places.

I live in London.
London is the special name of a city.

Noun	Special names/Proper nouns
street	Oak Lane
school	Montfort School
apartments	Royal Apartments
park	Yellow Stone Park
city	New York
state	Texas
country	France

Ronny wants to meet his friend. Draw lines to help him find his way to Royal Apartments from the park. Pick words from the box and write names of the places that fall on his way.

Palm Street, Lane Street, Regent Park, Royal Apartments, Mont Fort School, Club 65,

QUICK CHECK
Names of clubs, museums, hotels, malls and restaurants are also proper nouns.

Try it! Do you know your address? Write it here with the name of your country.

_____

_____

What day is it?

Proper nouns are also used to denote days, months and days like festivals and holidays.

Christmas is celebrated on 25th December every year.

This year Christmas falls on Sunday.

Birthday Time!

Write names of any of your 5 friends with their birthdays. Also write which day it is on their birthday.

Try it! List out three holidays or special days you will celebrate this year.

Terrific Titles!

Proper nouns also name titles of books, movies, television shows, plays and songs.

Have you read the book <u>Smith and Harry</u>?

I like to watch the cartoon <u>Tin-Tin</u>.

Rewrite the following sentences, put the underlined titles in capital letters.

QUICK CHECK
Words like and, the, a, of, when written between titles should not be written with capital letter. The first word of the title however begins with a capital letter.

1. Our family went to watch the <u>toy story</u>.

_____

2. Teacher read the story <u>the chocolate factory</u> to us.

_____

3. Sam likes to watch <u>pokemon</u>.

_____

4. We are going to act <u>the little mermaid</u>.

_____

Fill this about your mother. Don't forget to use capital letters where needed.

Name   _____

Her birthday   _____

Street Address   _____

City   _____

Title of favourite book   _____

Title of favourite TV show_____

Best Friend   _____

Favourite place to visit   _____

Action Words or Verbs

A verb is a word that denotes actions. It tells us what people, things, animals or creatures do.

Verbs also tell us what is happening.

I jump. I shake.

I dance. I hop.

I will move and not stop.

The words jump, shake, dance and hop show actions. They are verbs.

Circle the verb in each sentence.

1. Jane helps dad in the garden.
2. Dad mows the lawn.
3. Jane pulls the weeds.
4. Dad picks vegetables.
5. Then they paint the fence.
6. Dad gives her ice cream as a treat after dinner.

Use verbs from the box to complete the poem.

The Sun shines.   The birds _____.

The wind _____.   The river _____.

Rabbits _____.   Girls _____.

And We _____!

flows	chirp	blows	shines
	sing	stop	hop

Try it!

Write two sentences on how you help your Dad. Underline the verbs.

_____

_____

Is, Am, Are

The verbs, <u>is</u>, <u>am</u> and <u>are</u> tell us what things are like. They denote the time 'now'.

I <u>am</u> a girl.

My dress <u>is</u> clean.

My shoes <u>are</u> black.

Use <u>is</u>, <u>am</u> or <u>are</u> to fill in the blanks.

1. Robin _____ a baker.

2. Paul and John _____ his friends.

3. They _____ at Robin's bakery.

4. It _____ a cold morning today.

5. It _____ 8 o'clock. The men _____ hungry now.

6. Robin says, "I _____ hungry too."

7. The cookies _____ ready.

8. "We _____ happy now," say Paul and John.

Try it!

Write three sentences about yourself using is, am, are.

_____

_____

_____

Was, Were

The verbs <u>was</u> and <u>were</u> tell us what things were like in the past.

Peter <u>was</u> sad yesterday.

His toys <u>were</u> broken.

Use <u>was</u> or <u>were</u> to fill in the blanks.

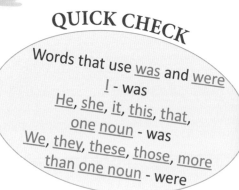

QUICK CHECK

Words that use <u>was</u> and <u>were</u>
<u>I</u> - was
<u>He</u>, <u>she</u>, <u>it</u>, <u>this</u>, <u>that</u>,
<u>one noun</u> - was
<u>We</u>, <u>they</u>, <u>these</u>, <u>those</u>, <u>more</u>
<u>than one noun</u> - were

1. It _____ music class on Monday.

2. Some children _____ late for the class.

3. Kim and Jacob _____ the first to come.

4. Pinto _____ the last to come.

5. We _____ in our seats soon.

6. Drums _____ in the class. We played them.

7. The teacher _____ pleased with us.

8. The boys and girls _____ happy.

Try it!

Write a sentence with the word 'flute' using <u>was</u> or <u>were</u>.

_____

_____

_____

Has, Have, Had

The verbs, <u>has</u>, <u>have</u> and <u>had</u> tell us that something belongs to someone.

Has and have are used in the present.

Peter <u>has</u> three books.

The girls <u>have</u> a pencil in their hand.

Had is used in the past.

Last year, Lucy <u>had</u> a toy car.

Use <u>has</u> or <u>have</u> to fill in the blanks.

1. Dane _____ two pet cats.

2. The cats _____ small ears.

3. One cat _____ white fur.

4. The other cat _____ brown fur.

5. Both cats _____ thin tails.

6. The brown cat _____ blue eyes.

7. The white cat _____ stripes.

Rewrite these sentences using <u>had</u>.

1. Jenny has a party yesterday. _____

2. She has a crown on her head. _____

3. Her friends have flowers on their hair. _____

Try it! Write two sentences about what you have in your school bag.

_____

_____

Pronouns

A pronoun is a word used in place of a noun. A pronoun must match the noun it replaces.

I, you, he, she and it are singular pronouns.

Sentences with nouns	Pronouns in place of nouns
Daniel has a football.	He has a football.
The football is big.	It is big.
Daniel's sister also plays with it.	She also plays with it.

QUICK CHECK
The pronoun I is always written in capitals. It is used for animals and things without life.

Pick and circle the correct pronoun to replace the underlined noun in each sentence.

1. Jason went on a trip to the Safari.   He   It

2. The Safari was hot and dry.   They   It

3. Jason's uncle saw a Prickly Pear.   He   It

4. The prickly pear does not have leaves.   We   It

5. Jason saw a Red Tegu!   She   He

6. A Red Tegu is a lizard found in Africa.   It   They

7. Jason was scared!   He   She

8. Jason's mother and father were a little scared, too.   They   We

Try it!

Write two sentences about an animal you are scared of. Use three pronouns in it.

_____

_____

Plural Pronouns

Pronouns <u>we</u>, <u>you</u> and <u>they</u> are plural pronouns. They are used in place of plural nouns.

<u>Sharks</u> are water animals.   <u>They</u> are water animals.

<u>Ronny and</u> I saw a shark.   <u>We</u> saw a shark.

Rewrite the sentences using pronouns in place of the underlined nouns.

1. <u>Jags and Nora</u> are going to the sea shore.

_____

QUICK CHECK

The pronoun <u>you</u> is used for both singular and plural nouns.

2. Did <u>Jags and Nora</u> see the shark?

_____

3. Sharks don't eat people, so <u>Jags and I</u> are not in danger.

_____

4. Mom and Jags want to see snails. <u>Snails</u> are so cute!

_____

5. "Have <u>Jags and Nora</u> ever seen a snail?" asked Mom.

_____

6. <u>Jags and Dad</u> also saw a crab.

_____

7. <u>Crabs</u> always walk sideways.

_____

8. "<u>Nora and I</u> are having so much fun on the shore," said Jags to mom.

_____

Try it!	What would you and your brother like to do at the sea shore? Write it using 'We'. _____ _____

I, We, Me and Us

We use <u>I</u> and <u>we</u> in the naming part of a sentence.
<u>I</u> like to dance.
<u>We</u> will wear frocks in the dance show.
We use <u>me</u> and <u>us</u> in the telling part of a sentence.
My mother is calling <u>me</u>.
The tailor will stitch the dress for <u>us</u>.

Rewrite the sentences using correct pronouns in place of underlined ones.

1. Mom and <u>me</u> went to see a magic show.

_____

QUICK CHECK
Name yourself last when talking about yourself and another person.

2. The usher gave <u>I</u> a ticket and showed <u>we</u> where to sit.

_____

3. <u>I</u> could see the rabbits coming out of the hat.

_____

4. <u>us</u> also saw paper flowers changing to roses.

_____

5. <u>Us</u> had great time!

_____

6. <u>me</u> hope Mom takes <u>I</u> to another show soon!

_____

Try it! | Write about a gift you got on your birthday. Write a sentence using I and me.

_____

_____

GRAMMAR 2

He, him/She, her

We use **he** and **him** to refer to a male and **she** and **her** to refer to a female.

1. Look at **Jack. He** is eating pasta.
2. Tell **him** to hurry up.
3. Today is **Jane's** birthday. **She** is 3 years old.
4. Don't buy a ticket for **her**.

Rewrite the sentences using he, she, him or her in place of the underlined nouns.

QUICK CHECK

We use **he** and **she** in naming part of a sentence. Whereas **him** and **her** are used in telling part of a sentence.

1. John asks Mary to help <u>John</u> choose a pet.

   _____

2. First John wanted a dog. Then <u>John</u> wanted a cat.

   _____

3. John said to <u>Mary</u>, "Cats don't need baths, they don't need walks."

   _____

4. <u>Mary</u> said, "Dogs like to play. They can learn tricks."

   _____

5. <u>John</u> talked to Mom and Dad. They asked <u>John</u> to take votes.

   _____

6. Tomorrow <u>John</u> is going to get a dog. We know exactly what kind.

   _____

Try it! | Write five sentences about your friends using he, him, she and her.

They-them

Read the sentences. Choose the correct pronoun from the parentheses to complete the sentence.

1. Jason and Nora are going to the Maldives. (We, They) are at the airport.

2. Other travellers walk in the airport. Nora wonders where (she, they) are going.

3. Some of (their, them) are excited.

4. Others look tired and bored. So (they, you) talk to each other.

5. Nora and Jason are in the queue.

   (Them, they) see the queue moving.

6. Jason goes to the clerks. (He, They)

   put Jason's bags on a moving belt.

7. The clerks give Jason and Nora (him, their) luggage.

8. The people were moving to the gate. (They, She) will soon board the plane.

Try it! Work with your friend and write your own dialogues using different kinds of pronoun.

Possessive Pronouns

A possessive pronoun shows who or what owns something.

For example:
Where is **his** bag?
Here is **her** book.

Read the pronouns and sort them using the colour code. Write them under the correct categories.

Possessive pronoun

Not a possessive pronoun

I
we
my
your
they
their

she
his
them
her
he

Colour code:

Possessive pronoun – blue

Not a possessive pronoun – orange

Possessive Pronouns–my, your, our

A possessive pronoun takes the place of a possessive noun.
A possessive pronoun shows who or what owns something.
My, your, his, her, its, our, your and their are
possessive pronouns.

For example:
This is **my** globe. This is **your** map.

Tick the correct possessive pronoun in the bracket for each sentence.

1. (Me, My) favourite explorer is Christopher Columbus.

2. (His, He) three ships were called the *Niña,
Pinta,* and *Santa Maria.*

3. (Him, His) most important discovery
was that of America.

4. (We, Our) teacher told us more about
Christopher's voyages.

5. In (he, his) calculations, Columbus
thought that Asia would be 2,400 miles
from Portugal.

6. I took (my, me) map and followed the
route.

7. Poppy is tracing his journey on
(her, their) map.

8. Sarah was the one to find the route in
(she, her) map.

Try it! | Which pronoun would you use to replace your name? Use the pronoun and its possessive form to make three sentences.

Possessive Pronouns- Its, our, your, their

Underline the possessive pronoun that completes each sentence correctly. Write it on the blank.

1. "I will show you _____ (my, me, I) new friends," said Tim.

2. Kayla wanted to show off _____ (she, her, its) unusual friend too.

3. Sammy climbed up and put _____ (his, you, me) hand on the branch.

4. "Should we cover _____ (her, my, our) eyes?" Ina asked.

5. "Hold on to _____ (your, its, their) hats, friends!" Tim said with a grin.

6. _____ (your, its, our) friends are not like other usual friends," Sally said.

7. "What's in _____ (me, their, its) pouch?" Kayla asked.

8. "_____ (their, his, its) pouch is to nourish the baby" Tim said.

Possessive Pronouns

Circle the incorrect use of possessive pronouns in the sentences below. Write them correctly.

1. What is yours favourite thing to do in summer vacation?

2. Mine family visits a different theme park every summer.

3. Yang has his' own idea of building a theme park.

4. There would be only roller coasters in his's.

5. Millie said that her would have water rides and a veggie park.

6. I would have a mix of everything in mine's.

7. That ride is fun because of it's fast speed.

8. Next vacation my parents and I will visit ours favourite theme park.

QUICK CHECK

Mine, his, yours, theirs are also possessive pronouns. They refer to the nouns in subject.

Try it! Use the pronouns my and mine in sentences of your own.

Subject-Verb Agreement

A verb must agree with a noun or pronoun in the subject part of a sentence. A singular subject takes a singular verb and a plural subject takes a plural verb.

Example:
He picks a flower.
They smell the rose.

Fill in the blanks with the correct form of verbs.

1. We _____ food at the new cafe. (buy, buys)

2. I _____ at the menu first. (look, looks)

3. It _____ us different things available at the cafe. (tell, tells)

4. She_____ the beverages section in the menu. (read, reads).

5. We _____ juice and shakes the most. (like, likes)

6. He _____ sandwich and juice. (choose, chooses)

7. I _____ to have fruits too. (want, wants)

8. The food _____yummy. It is healthy too. (taste, tastes)

QUICK CHECK

We add –s or –es to the verbs when the pronoun is singular. Adding –s or –es also denote that the action is happening in the present.

Subject-Verb Agreement

Write the verb that completes each sentence. Colour the matching hearts.

1. Susane and Pam _____ making cards for their parents.

2. They _____ a lot of cards to make.

3. Now Susane _____ cutting out hearts.

4. She _____ some red and white paper.

5. Pam _____ a handful of glitter to add to each one.

6. The hearts _____ red and golden.

7. The glitter _____ shiny.

8. Each card _____ a nice note on it.

9. Pam _____ an envelope for each card.

10. The cards _____ special because they are handmade.

Try it! Choose three nouns or pronouns from this page. Write each one in a sentence with a different verb.

Subject-Verb Agreement

Circle the word that completes each sentence.

1. We (grow, grows) pumpkins on our farm.

2. My father (plant, plants) the seeds in spring season.

3. My mother and I (watch, watches) the little plants all summer long.

QUICK CHECK

We use **am, is, was** and **have** with the pronoun I. **Is, am** and **was** are used with singular pronoun and have with plural pronouns. Use of **have** with **I** is exceptional.

4. The bees (buzz, buzzes) around the pumpkin blossoms.

5. In a few days, the first pumpkin (begin, begins) to grow.

6. We (help, helps) dad to pick the pumpkins.

7. I (choose, chooses) one pumpkin and carry it into the house.

8. Mom cuts it into pieces and (scoop, scoops).

9. Then she (bake, bakes) a pumpkin pie.

10. All of us (love, loves) pumpkin pie.

Pronoun-Verb Agreement

Read the paragraph and find the mistakes. Then rewrite the paragraph correctly.

Dad and I goes to the library. He read how to grow carrots. I reads *A Kid's Guide to Gardening*. The book tell us how to grow a garden. We wants to plant carrots, beans and potatoes. We knows it takes hard work. For a while, it seem that nothing happens. We waits patiently, and soon green shoots appear. One day I sees some white blossoms. I like gardening.

_____

_____

_____

_____

_____

_____

Contractions

A contraction is a short form of two words put together. An apostrophe (')
takes the place of the letter or letters that are left out. Some contractions
are formed by putting together pronouns and verbs.

Example:

I am   I'm   she is   she's   he is   he's

Circle the words in bold. Write the contractions.

1. **We will** take care of the earth.   _____
2. **We are** planting many trees.   _____
3. **It is** good to pick up litter.   _____
4. **He will** turn off the lights.   _____
5. **Let us** take a bike instead of a car.   _____
6. **Who will** recycle cardboard boxes today? _____
7. **They have** been recycling newspapers.   _____
8. **You are** a friend of the earth!   _____

Word bank	
you're	we'll
they've	It's
we're	let's
he'll	who's

Contractions

Circle the contraction that completes each sentence. Then write it on the blank.

1. _____ forget the car keys.

2. I think _____ beautiful.

3. The flowers _____ wrapped.

4. _____ the red blossom.

5. We _____ have any orchids.

6. She _____ want tulips.

7. They _____ been watered.

8. This _____ my vase.

9. _____ working today?

10. _____ a great flower shop.

Don't	Dont'
Its	it's
aren't	arent'
There's	theres
didn't	did'nt
doesnt	doesn't
haven't	havent'
Isn't	isn't
Who's	whos
That's	that's

QUICK CHECK

Remember that an apostrophe takes the place of the letter or letters that are left out of a contraction. Apostrophe is always used with the second word. Like- have not will be written as haven't and not hav'nt.

Contractions

Possessive pronouns, such as **their**, **your**, and **its** do not have apostrophes.

Possessive Pronoun
its
their
your

Contraction
you're
it's
they're

Read each sentence. Write the correct pronoun or contraction on the line.

1. (They're, Their)_____ teacher is teaching a lesson about the moon.

2. (Their, They're) _____reading the book Rocket to the Moon.

3. (Its, It's) _____about the first landing on the moon.

4. Are they almost finished with _____(they're their) book?

5. (Your, You're)_____ reading a book called The Moon.

6. What is (your, you're) _____book about?

7. The book is about the moon and (it's, its) _____phases.

8. (Its, It's)_____ full of interesting facts.

Contractions

Read the paragraph. Circle any incorrectly written contractions.

...m Rosa. I want to become a zoologist. Thats someone who studies animals. ...ntil then I will learn about animals by watching and reading.

...here are plenty of rabbits in our backyard. Theyve built their warren near ...ne fence. Ive seen rabbits hop across the yard. Then suddenly theyre gone ...down the hole into the warren. I cant go down there! So I read about what ...s like inside. Then I drew a picture of it.

_____

_____

_____

_____

_____

_____

_____

_____

_____

Try it! Rewrite the paragraph by placing each contraction with the apostrophe in the right place. Use possessive pronouns and contractions correctly.

Adjectives

Adjectives are words that describe people, places, animals and things.
Example:
The eucalyptus tree is **tall**.
I see a **blue** balloon flying high.

Choose the best adjectives for each ad below and complete it.

Lost Dog	Please help me find my _____ (tiny, cute) dog. It is _____ (brown, black) with a _____ (dark, light) patch on his tummy. His fur is _____ (hairy, smooth) and his tail is _____ (fuzzy, long). My dog is very _____ (scary, friendly). I miss my dog!
Call Miss Sara 333-0033	
Lost Dog	Please help me find my _____ (huge, little) dog. It is _____ (pretty, white) with _____ (black, brown) spots on it. It has _____ (long, short) ears. Its legs are _____ (slender, small). It has a _____ (white, striped) collar around its neck. I miss my dog!
Call Mr. Ron 666-1231	

Adjectives—What Kind

Some adjectives tell what kind.

For example:

pink balloons   **big** balloons

Fill in the blanks with adjectives. Use the word bank.

1. Sail around the _____ island and past the _____ ship.

2. Land on the _____ side of Secret Island.

3. Walk onto the sandy beach and around the _____ cactus.

4. Wade across the _____ pond.

5. Then hike to the _____ cave.

6. Look for the _____ rock that looks like a ball.

7. Take _____, _____ steps toward the _____ tree.

8. Dig a _____ hole until you hit something _____ like metal.

Word Bank
round
hard
west
small
sunken
deep
prickly
shallow
tallest
dark
triangular

Try it! Write directions from your classroom to the nearest water fountain.
Underline each adjective you use.

Adjectives–How Many

We use some adjectives to tell how many.

Example:

I saw **three** squirrels on the tree.

Please give me **a few** envelopes.

Circle the adjectives that tell how many. Then rewrite each sentence using another adjective.

1. Sally's birthday is in three weeks.

   _____

2. She is inviting ten friends to her birthday party.

   _____

3. Her brother Sam is blowing up a few balloons.

   _____

4. There will be nine candles on her cake.

   _____

5. One candle is for good luck.

   _____

6. There will be many sweet
   treats in the party.

   _____

Try it! | Look around and write down names of ten things you see. Use adjectives to describe them.

Comparison of Adjectives

We can use adjectives to compare people, places or things. Add -er to an adjective to compare two nouns.

Example:

This pencil is longer than that pencil.

Big	Bigger	Biggest
Long	Longer	Longest

Add –er to the adjectives and complete the table.

Adjective	Add – er	Adjective	Add – er
Small		Tall	
Warm		Cool	
Bright		Thick	
Hard		Long	
Soft		Thin	
Smart		Slow	
Quiet		Dark	

Comparison of Adjectives

Fill in the blanks with the correct form of the adjectives.

1. Hammy's Hat Store is a _____ (new, newer) store in the city.

2. The prices at his store are _____(low, lower) than prices in the town.

3. The fur hats are _____ (warm, warmer) than the other hats.

4. They are _____(soft, softer) than the straw hats.

5. The straw hats are _____(cheap, cheaper) and nice.

6. They are also _____(small, smaller) than the cowboy hats.

7. The cowboy hats have a _____(high, higher) price.

8. _____(wide, wider) hats in the store have flowers on them.

9. It is _____ (nice, nicer) than the straw hats.

10. Hammy keeps her store _____ (clean, cleaner) and tidy.

QUICK CHECK

Adjectives that end in –er are usually used with than. We also don't use articles a or an with them.

Comparison of Adjectives

Write the adjectives that complete each sentence.
Then circle the adjective in the puzzle.

1. The children are dressed for
   the_____ costume party.
   (grander, grandest)

2. The fairy is _____ than the
   clown. (taller, tallest)

3. The clown's laugh is _____ than
   the cowboy's laugh. (louder, loudest)

4. The fairy has the _____
   costume at the party. (fancier,
   fanciest)

5. The pirate is _____than the
   fairy. (plump, plumper)

6. The fairy wants the _____
   apple in the basket. (smaller,
   smallest)

7. The cowboy's bag of candy is
   _____ than the pirate's.
   (bigger, biggest)

8. These are the _____party
   guests. (happier, happiest)

```
A  Z  Y  P  L  U  M  P  E  R

T  K  C  N  B  I  G  G  E  R

S  V  R  E  D  U  O  L  S  K

E  S  M  A  L  L  E  S  T  D

D  O  F  A  N  C  I  E  S  T

N  T  I  J  T  D  F  B  L  Q

A  T  S  E  I  P  P  A  H  K

R  N  D  H  V  D  A  S  P  H

G  P  P  V  O  E  L  K  O  Y

R  E  L  L  A  T  V  F  B  N
```

Try it! Write a few sentences on a fancy costume party. Use adjectives to compare the people at the party.

Adjectives That Compare

Add –er or –est to the base word and write the adjective on the blank.

1. Bella thinks tennis is the _____ sport of all. (great)

2. Her new racquet is _____ than her old one. (light)

3. She can swing the new racquet _____ than the old one. (fast)

4. Now her serves are _____ than her brother's. (quick)

5. She is still the _____ player on the team. (young)

6. But she is also the _____ of them all! (fast)

7. The other team's player is _____ than Bella. (tall)

8. But she has practiced _____ than he has! (hard)

9. Bella wants to be the _____ player in her school. (great)

10. She hopes to win the _____ trophy she has ever won. (big)

Try it! Write three sentences using adjectives on this page. Write them in the –est form.

Adverbs

An **adverb is a word that** tells more about a verb.
An adverb can tell how, when and where.

Example:

The bird flew **swiftly**.
The word **swiftly** tells how the bird flew.

QUICK CHECK

Adverbs that tell how usually end in –ly. We can form such adverbs by adding –ly to adjectives.
Loud + ly = loudly
Soft + ly = softly

Circle the verb in each sentence. Then write the adverb on the line.

1. Julia spoke enthusiastically about her robot to the class.

   _____

2. Everyone listened carefully to her.

   _____

3. Henry pulled the lever gently.

   _____

4. The robot moved suddenly and walked around.

   _____

5. The students cheered loudly for the robot.

   _____

6. The clever robot bowed gracefully.

   _____

Try it! Think of any 5 adjectives. Add –ly to each and change it to an adverb.

Adverbs

Underline the verb in each sentence. Then circle the adverb and write it on the chart below.

1. Rosh walks toward a sleeping lion.
2. He firmly holds his camera.
3. Lee hides behind Rosh.
4. Yesterday, Lee scared a dog.
5. Today, Lee remembers to be quiet.
6. The lion quietly moves one eye.
7. Now Rex takes a picture.
8. The lion roars loudly.
9. Lee and Rosh stand still.
10. Lee and Rosh sneak away.

How?	When?	Where?

Using Adverbs

Write a sentence about each picture. Use the adverb.

1. playfully _____

_____

2. carefully _____

_____

3. quickly _____

_____

4. neatly _____

_____

5. lovingly _____

_____

6. slowly _____

_____

Adverbs That Tell How

Read the sentences about Nancy's garden. In each sentence, circle the adverb that tells how. Then write the adverb in the matching space.

1. Nancy absolutely loves gardening.
2. She mostly grows carrots and lettuce.
3. When spring arrives, Nancy carefully plans her garden.
4. She plants very tiny seeds.
5. Then she quickly waters the soil.
6. Every day, Nancy works to keep other insects from greedily eating her plants.
7. Months later, she lovingly admires her garden.
8. Then Nancy gently picks her vegetables and shares them with her friends.

1.
2.
3.
4.
5.
6.
7.
8.

What type of insect is aphid? To find out match the circled letter in each word to a line below.

___ ___ ___ ___ ___ ___ ___ ___
7   3   6   4   1   5   8   2

GRADE 2: GRAMMAR 2

Adverbs That Tell When

We also use adverbs to tell when.

Example:

I painted a picture **yesterday.**

Read each sentence. Choose the adverb that tells when.

1. Linda wakes up _____. (early, peacefully)

2. She takes her morning walk_____ (slowly, first)

3. _____ she eats breakfast and hurries back outside. (quickly, then)

4. _____ she gets her gardening tools. (happily, next)

5. She's ready to start working _____. (hard, now)

6. Linda will _____ leave a weed in her garden. (not, never)

7. She works _____ every day. (busily, late)

8. She waters the plants _____. (last, deeply)

Using Adverbs

Write a sentence using each adverb.

1. Outside _____

   _____

2. Today _____

   _____

3. Everywhere _____

   _____

4. Never _____

   _____

5. Long ago _____

   _____

6. Finally _____

   _____

7. Often _____

   _____

Using Nouns, Adjectives and Adverbs

Look at the picture and write a paragraph on it. Use three nouns, three adjectives and three adverbs in the paragraph.

_____

_____

_____

_____

_____

_____

Fun With Adjectives

Directions: For each word roll a dice and add -er or -est accordingly.

 **-er**

If you roll 1, 2, or 3, add on -er ending to the word.

 **-est**

If you roll 4, 5, or 6, add on -er ending to the word.

Read Word	Roll	Answer
cute		
old		
easy		
high		
grumpy		
thin		
smart		
sweet		
kind		
scary		
small		

Read Word	Roll	Answer
tall		
soft		
bright		
dry		
tasty		
silly		
funny		
great		
quick		
full		
short		

WRITING

Writing a Title

A title is a word or group of words that describe what a picture, text or story is about.

Titles:
- are interesting
- are short
- tell what the picture is about

Choose a Title

What is each picture about? Circle the best title.

1. Hot Sun
   My New Umbrella
   A Sunny Day

2. Big and Small Cars
   Going to School
   Too Much Traffic

3. Run and Run
   Running a Race
   Big Shoes

Write a Title

Write a title to tell what each picture is about.

1. _____

2. _____

3. _____

What Is Happening?

What is happening in these pictures? Write some sentences of your own to describe these pictures.

_____

_____

_____

> **QUICK CHECK**

Make sure each sentence begins with a capital letter and ends with a period.

_____

_____

_____

Using Describing Words in Writing

A detail is a small piece of information that helps readers know about what we write. We use describing words to add detail to our text. Describing words tell us how something looks, feels, sounds, smells or tastes.

Yesterday, Neo went to see penguins. He wrote:

Penguins have legs.

Neo did not use describing words to write about the penguin's legs. We can add a word to help the reader know about the penguin's legs.

short

Penguins have ˄ legs.

Read Neo's sentences about penguins. Add describing words to the sentences where you find this symbol (˄).

1. The penguin is a ˄ bird.

2. It has a ˄ body.

3. It has ˄ feathers than most birds.

4. Penguins are ˄ swimming birds.

5. They are ˄ birds and are found in groups.

Using Describing Words in Writing

Look at the pictures. Write some sentences about them using describing words. The first one for each picture has been done for you.

Brian got soap water for making bubbles.

_____

_____

_____

_____

Mother bought a new bike for Kelly.

_____

_____

_____

_____

Write a detail

Now write some sentences about your visit to the market last time. Answer each question. Include at least one describing word in each sentence.

1. What did you see in the market? Was it big, small or many?

_____

2. What did you hear? Were the sounds loud or soft?

_____

3. What did you buy? Was it bumpy, hard, soft?

_____

4. Did you have something to eat? How did it taste?

_____

5. How did you feel to go to the market? Tired, fun or happy?

_____

Things to Do!

We do many things every day. There are some things that
we do every day. On other days, we do different things. It is
fun to write about what we do.

What do you do every day? Make a list of tasks
and write them below.

1. _____

2. _____

3. _____

4. _____

5. _____

6. _____

7. _____

8. _____

9. _____

10. _____

Things to Do

Write some sentences about what you have done today.

Remember to put the events in order.

_____

_____

_____

_____

_____

_____

Write about Sunday.

Now, write some sentences about what you do on a Sunday.

_____

_____

_____

_____

I Feel...

How do you feel today? Pick words from the word bank. Draw a picture that shows how you feel.

	Word Bank
	Sad
	Happy
	Excited
	Nervous
	Anxious
	Eager
	Overjoyed
	Good
	Dull

Now write 2–3 sentences about how you feel. Add details about why you feel this way.

_____

_____

_____

_____

_____

_____

How Do You Feel?

Imagine it is your birthday and you have a party planned. How do you feel?
Draw a picture. Then write 5 sentences telling how you feel.

Pretend that you participated in a race or game. You tried hard but did not
win. How would you feel? Draw a picture and write a few sentences about it.

Writing About Places

Daniel wrote a few sentences about his room. Read them.

1. The room is big and has walls.

2. There is some furniture in the room.

3. There is a cupboard to keep things.

4. There are lots of things on the shelf.

5. I decorate my room with balloons on my birthday.

He did not write details about some things.

For example: In the first sentence, Daniel has written about the size of the room but what do "many things" look like? We cannot understand because we do not know what these things are.

Let's write a new sentence to describe Daniel's room.

    1. The room is big and has green walls.

Now we know what is colour is the wall.

Use words to describe just what you want the readers to know about Daniel's room.

1. _____

2. _____

3. _____

4. _____

5. _____

Now write about your room. Add as many details as you can.

_____

_____

_____

_____

_____

_____

_____

_____

Writing About a Place You Visited

You must have visited a park, a restaurant and a market. Write a few sentences about any one place. Use details to help the readers know about the place.

_____

_____

_____

_____

_____

_____

_____

Quick Check

Look back at your sentences. Do they start with a capital letter and end with a period? Do they have all necessary details about the place you have written.

I Can Imagine

What if you could create a new park? Would your park have different swings? Would it have fountains, picnic tables, barbeque grills? Close your eyes and imagine your new park. Write some words that tell what you "see" in this park.

_____

_____

_____

Imagine your park again. What colours do you see? What do you hear and smell? What do different things feel like? Write some sentences that tell what things in your park look, feel, sound and smell like.

_____

_____

_____

GRADE 2: WRITING

Write What You Think

Imagine it is a rainy Sunday. What will you do? Use the word bank to write sentences of your own.

Word Bank

ball   car   dog

pizza   book   cat

hat   puddle   boots

coat   house   towel

When Did It Happen?

Look at the pictures below. Write **first, next** and **last**. These are called **time-order words**.

_____

_____

_____

_____

When Did It Happen?

Now write sentences to show the order of events. Write one sentence about each picture.

First, _____.

Next, _____.

Last, _____.

First, _____.

Next, _____.

Last, _____.

When Did It Happen?

In a story, we usually tell what happens in order. First, one thing happens. Then, another thing happens, and so on.

Write what is happening in these pictures. Then, add more sentences and write what happened next and at last for these pictures.

_____

_____

_____

_____

_____

_____

_____

_____

_____

What Is a Story?

A story tells about people, places or animals. A good story is interesting for the reader to read. It also has **describing words** that tell us about the characters, where the story takes place and what happens.

A story has:

- some characters
- a beginning, a middle and an end

Read the story carefully. Think about what happens at the beginning and in the middle.

Polly Makes a Snake

Mac and Polly are camping in the yard. They have their flashlights and some tasty snacks. Mac swings his flashlight around in the big tent. Hoot! Hoot! He makes scary noises. Polly is not scared. She remembers what she learnt in school about shadows. A solid object in front of light makes a shadow.

She shines her flashlight on the side of the tent. She puts her hand in front of the light. She twists her hand around. "Look, a snake!" Polly says. Mac jumps. Then he sees that it is only a shadow. They laugh and laugh together.

Read the story again. Can you find the ending of the story? Underline it.

Answer these questions about the story *Polly Makes a Snake*. Look back on page 22 if you need.

1. Who are the characters in the story?

_____   _____

2. What happens at the beginning, in the middle and at the end of the story?

Beginning

Middle

End

3. Which words are used to describe the tent, snacks and noises? Can you use some other describing words for these words?

_____

_____

_____

Writing the Title of a Story

The title of a story tells us what the story is about.

Ollie is an owl. It has big eyes. Ollie's wings have soft feathers. Ollie can see well in the dark and likes to hunt at night. "I can turn my head almost all the way around." Ollie says. That helps Ollie find animals. Ollie has sharp claws too. They help it catch small animals. Ollie has a strong beak. The beak helps it carry its food.

1. What is the best title for the story? Circle your choice.
A. Ollie's Day   B. Ollie, the owl   C. Ollie hunts at night

Paula visits Farmer Jack's pumpkin farm. It is a huge field of pumpkins. The pumpkins grow on vines. Farmer Jack shows her a perfect pumpkin.

"This is the stem," he says. "It is attached to the vine."

The outside of the pumpkin is the rind and the lines are called ribs. He cuts the pumpkin in half. Paula touches the seeds and pulp inside. It is sticky and gooey! Farmer Jack gives her

roasted pumpkin seeds. They are crunchy!

2. What is the best title for the story? Circle your choice.
A. Mixed up day   B. Perfect Pumpkin
C. Paula at the Pumpkin Farm

Writing Title of a Story

Read the stories given below. Choose the best title for each story from the help box and write it on the line.

Dog and Ball, My Pet Jilly, A Helicopter Ride, Flying Helicopter

_____

I have a dog. Her name is Jilly. She loves to play catch. She uses her teeth to pick the ball I throw. Then she runs to me and gives me the ball. She raises her ears when she hears a voice. Jilly barks if she sees a stranger. She barks loudly to protect me.

_____

Kim and his mother went to an airport. "Those helicopters are huge!" Kim said. "Helicopters can land in small places," said his mother. "They can also fly side to side." A man came over. "I can take you for a ride in one," he said.
Sam and his mother buckled up. The blades of the helicopter spun around. Whirr! Whirr! Up went the helicopter. Kim looked down at his town. It was a great ride!

Writing a Story

Look at the picture. Think of a story you might write about the people or the place in the picture.

The people in the picture are the characters of your story. Think of names for them.

_____   _____

_____   _____

_____   _____

Write where these people are. You can also add describing words to tell about sounds, objects, smells, sights and colours.

_____   _____

_____   _____

_____   _____

_____   _____

Look at the picture on page 115 again. Write interesting things that you think will happen in the beginning, in the middle and at the end of your story.

Beginning

Middle

End

Now write your complete story here. Think of all the ideas you wrote on pages 115 and 116. Give your story a title. Use lots of describing words to make your story interesting.

_____

_____

_____

_____

_____

_____

_____

_____

_____

_____

_____

_____

It's Fun to Tell

It is fun to tell about things that we see or that happen—an interesting bird, a football game, your birthday party, a visit to the zoo or your garden.

Make notes about a visit to the zoo. Write about interesting things you saw there. First write down a few things to keep your ideas in order. Then write about what you saw in detail.

Notes

Went to the zoo

Many wild animals

Tiger then panda

Big ostrich eggs

No teasing

_____

_____

_____

_____

_____

_____

_____

The Writing Procss: Telling About People

My Best Friend

Write ten sentences to tell your parents about your best friend. Add a lot of information about him/her. You can take the help of the hint box.

- How old is he?
- Where does he live?
- What are his hobbies?
- Is he kind?
- How helpful is he?

- Which games does he like to play?
- Why do you like him?
- Do you quarrel?
- How do you spend time with him?

_____

_____

_____

_____

_____

_____

_____

_____

_____

The Writing Process: Facts and Opinions

A **fact** tells us something that is true and can be proven.

An **opinion** tells us how a person feels about something. It might tell that you like or dislike something.

For example:

A lion is a wild animal. (Fact)

Lion is the most wonderful animal. (Opinion)

Pick any two topics from the box alongside and write some facts about them.

Tiger
The Game Football
Summer Season
Ice Creams
A Pond
Zoo

_____

_____

_____

_____

_____

Now write 3–4 sentences that show your opinion on the topic you wrote above.

_____

_____

_____

_____

_____

My Favourite Story

Think of stories you have read. Write their titles on the lines below.

Stories on animals

_____

_____

Stories on prince and princesses

_____

_____

Magical stories

_____

_____

Adventure stories

_____

_____

Look at the story titles. Which one do you like the best?
Draw a star beside its title. Now write about
the story in short and why you find it the best.

_____

_____

_____

_____

_____

_____

_____

_____

_____

Writing a Story

Which fairy tale do you like the most? Write it in words of your own.

_____

_____

_____

_____

_____

_____

_____

_____

_____

_____

_____

_____

_____

_____

_____

_____

_____

_____

FUNDAMENTAL MATHS

Numbers to 999

Study the grid carefully.

10	20	30	40	50	60	70	80	90	100
110	120	130	140	150	160	170	180	190	200
210	220	230	240	250	260		280	290	300
310	320	330	340	350	360	370	380	390	400
410		430	440	450	460	470	480	490	500
510	520	530	540		560	570	580	590	600
610	620	630	640	650	660	670	680	690	
710	720	730	740	750	760		780	790	800
810	820	830	840	850	860	870	880	890	900
910		930	940	950	960	970	980	990	1000

1. Write the 6 missing numbers in the grid.

2. Write the numbers between 520 to 530.

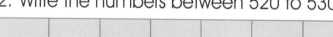

3. 5 more than 270.

4. 10 less than 580.

5. Write the numbers 10 more than 500, 760, 910, 650.

GRADE 2: FUNDAMENTAL MATHS

Modelling Numbers

Count the blocks and write the number. Also name the matching room.

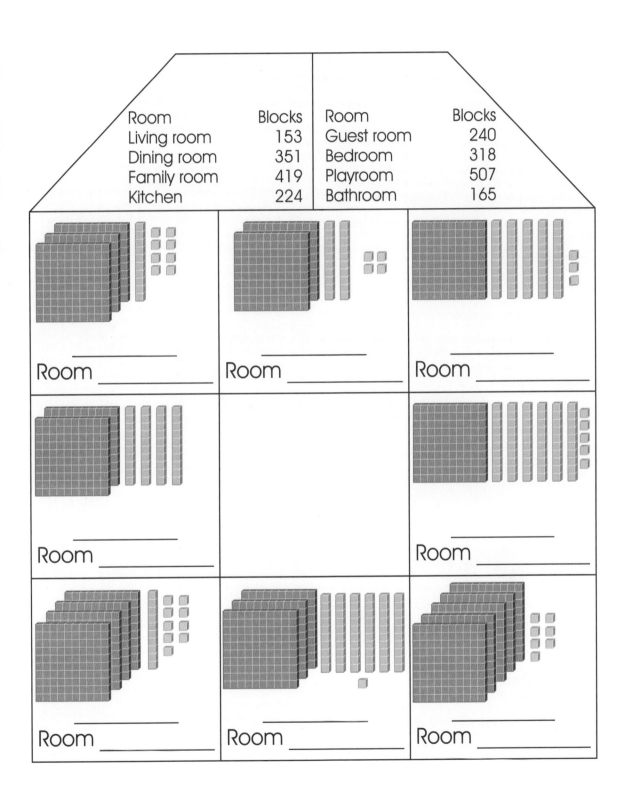

Room	Blocks	Room	Blocks
Living room	153	Guest room	240
Dining room	351	Bedroom	318
Family room	419	Playroom	507
Kitchen	224	Bathroom	165

Room _____

Room _____

Room _____

Room _____

Room _____

Room _____

Room _____

Room _____

Modelling Numbers

In each row, circle the blocks to show the number.

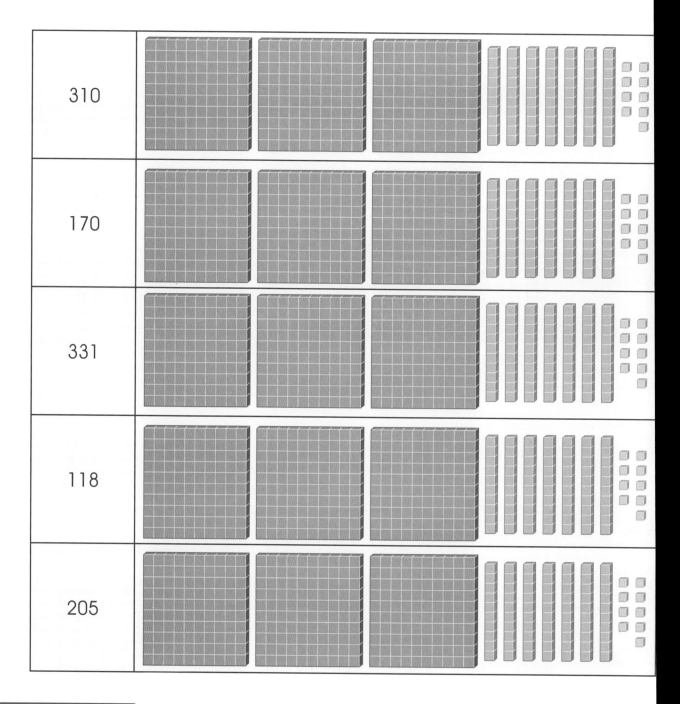

310		
170		
331		
118		
205		

Hundreds, Tens and Ones

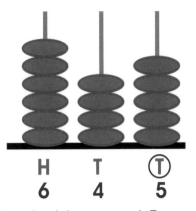

H T (T)
6 4 5

6 hundreds 4 tens and 5 ones

Write the number you see on each abacus.

①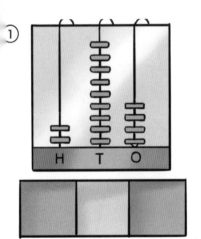

②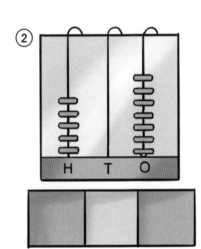

③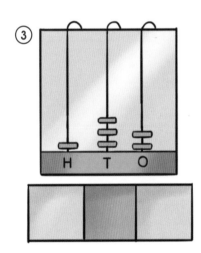

④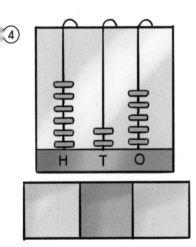

⑤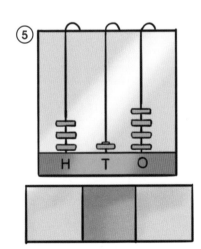

⑥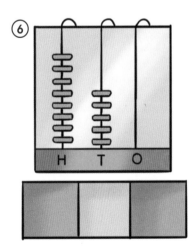

Before, Between and After

Write the numbers and complete the table.

Before		After
	339	
	517	
	208	
	899	
	700	

209
518
338
340
516
207
701
699
898
900
148
513
400
629
766
772

CHALLENGE

Make a grid of numbers such that each row adds up to 540.

	Between	
399		401
628		630
147		149
512		514
765		767
771		773

GRADE 2: FUNDAMENTAL MATHS

Place Value

Place value is the position of a digit in a number.

5<u>6</u>3 – The place value of 6 in 563 is 6 tens.

563
6 tens

Write the value of each underlined digit. Use the help box.

1. <u>3</u>8

   _____

2. 5<u>3</u>2

   _____

3. 4<u>6</u>0

   _____

4. <u>1</u>39

   _____

5. <u>7</u>40

   _____

6. <u>8</u>34

   _____

7. <u>5</u>59

   _____

8. 41<u>9</u>

   _____

9. 47<u>5</u>

   _____

10. 8<u>0</u>9

    _____

11. <u>9</u>28

    _____

12. 48<u>9</u>

    _____

13. <u>3</u>15

    _____

14. 92<u>2</u>

    _____

15. <u>6</u>01

    _____

16. 6<u>5</u>7

    _____

17. <u>4</u>95

    _____

18. 6<u>4</u>8

    _____

Place Value

Read each clue and find
the 3-digit number hidden in the
picture. Circle the number and write on the line.

1. There is a 8 in hundreds place and 3 in the tens place.

    <u>843</u>

2. There is a 4 in the hundreds place. The other two digits are the same.

    _____

3. The same digit is in hundreds place and the ones place.

    _____

4. There is a 6 in the tens place. The sum of the other two digits is 5.

    _____

5. There is a 9 in the ones place.

    _____

6. There is a 7 in the hundreds place.

    _____

7. There is a 4 in the tens place. The sum of the three digits is 16.

    _____

8. There is a 5 in the tens place.

    _____

7 6 2 (8 4 3) 2 6 9 7 2 7 4 5 5 6 0

Expanded Form of Numbers

Expanded form is a way to write a number that shows the place value for each place.

100 + **20** + **3**

Hundred   Tens   Ones

Write the expanded form of each number.

. 487 = _____ + _____ + _____

. 329 = _____ + _____ + _____

. 892 = _____ + _____ + _____

. 278 = _____ + _____ + _____

. 165 = _____ + _____ + _____

. 723 = _____ + _____ + _____

. 735 = _____ + _____ + _____

. 818 = _____ + _____ + _____

. 695 = _____ + _____ + _____

0. 224 = _____ + _____ + _____

CHALLENGE

Which number is smaller 600+90+8 or 689? Explain how?

Expanded Form of Numbers ◀

Write each number for the expanded form.

1. 400+60+9 = _____

2. 600+70+8 = _____

3. 900+50+4 = _____

4. 800+0+9 = _____

5. 500+10+4 = _____

6. 600+20+9 = _____

7. 100+80+0 = _____

8. 700+50+4 = _____

9. 300+80+8 = _____

10. 500+80+1 = _____

11. 200+70+3 = _____

12. 400+50+5 = _____

13. 100+90+9 = _____

14. 700+0+4 = _____

400 + 60 + 9

Expanded Form of Numbers

Write each number to its matching expanded form.

1. 7 hundreds

   6 tens   =

   4 ones

2. 5 hundreds

   3 tens   =

   6 ones

3. 8 hundreds

   1 ten   =

   8 ones

4. 9 hundreds

   2 tens   =

   3 ones

5. 4 hundreds

   3 tens   =

   8 ones

6. 8 hundreds

   3 tens   =

   9 ones

7. 5 hundreds

   0 tens   =

   3 ones

8. 6 hundreds

   9 tens   =

   7 ones

503	818	697	923
438	764	839	536

Comparing Numbers

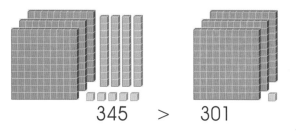

345 > 301

The symbol > points to the

number that is less

345 > 301 or 301 < 345

Write the number for each group. Compare the numbers with >, < or =.

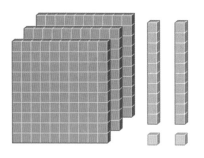

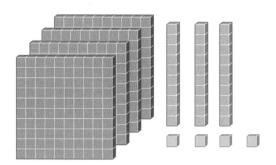

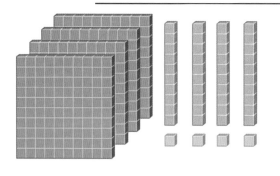

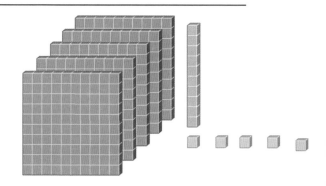

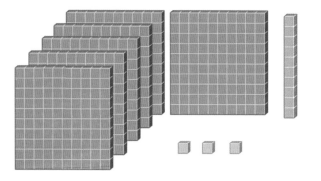

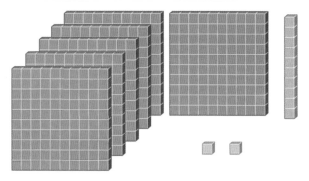

GRADE 2: FUNDAMENTAL MATHS

Comparing Numbers

Circle the matching number to make the comparison true. Write it on the line.

_____ > 335	_____ = 809	745 > _____
271 411 126	796 334 809	816 927 612
753 > _____	527 < _____	_____ > 241
886 522 935	421 891 344	254 457 119
_____ < 651	817 > _____	_____ = 976
625 894 753	998 218 827	220 976 429
_____ > 784	_____ < 876	475 > _____
658 998 218	786 966 899	980 337 567

CHALLENGE

Complete the puzzle.

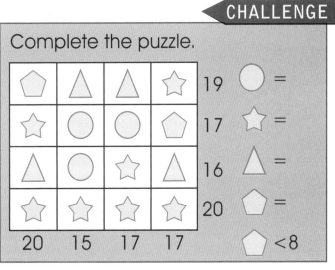

Comparing Numbers

Decide whether each number sentence is true.

Colour the matching star.

		YES	NO
1.	3 hundreds + 8 tens + 9 ones > 398	☆	☆
2.	748 = 7 hundreds + 4 tens + 8 ones	☆	☆
3.	2 hundreds + 6 ones = 260	☆	☆
4.	629 < 6 hundreds + 2 hundreds + 9 ones	☆	☆
5.	8 hundreds + 6 tens + 1 one > 8 hundreds + 1 ten and 8 ones	☆	☆
6.	9 hundreds + 5 tens + 6 ones > 953	☆	☆
7.	5 hundreds + 8 tens + 0 ones = 508	☆	☆
8.	4 hundreds + 3 tens + 2 ones < 443	☆	☆

CHALLENGE

Using the numbers 7, 5, 4 make as many numbers as you can.
Then make a chart comparing all these numbers.

GRADE 2: FUNDAMENTAL MATHS

Ordering Numbers

Read each set of numbers.
Write the numbers in
order from the least to the
greatest.

576
561
516

_____ , _____ , _____

343
324
334

_____ , _____ , _____

602
620
260

_____ , _____ , _____

131
101
113

_____ , _____ , _____

734
740
729

_____ , _____ , _____

830
800
893

_____ , _____ , _____

Writing Number Words

Write number words for these given numbers.

1. 679 _____

2. 342 _____

3. 908 _____

556

**Five hundred
and fifty six**

4. 556 _____

5. 876 _____

6. 259 _____

7. 445 _____

8. 178 _____

9. 784 _____

10. 119 _____

Counting in 5s and 10s

Write 5 more than:

1. 20 _____   2. 30 _____   3. 45 _____

4. 0 _____   5. 15 _____   6. 40 _____

7. 25 _____   8. 10 _____   9. 50 _____

10. 35 _____   11. 55 _____   12. 5 _____

Write the above numbers in order from least to greatest.

The numbers on the cards below are to be counted in 10s. Put the numbers in order from largest to smallest and complete the number grid. Write the missing numbers if any.

105	215	245	305	265	195	235
275	205	165	115	155	185	225

Counting in 2s, 3s, 4s, 5s, and 10s

Fill in the missing letters to complete the set of numbers. Write the rule you used.

1. ☐ , ☐ , 130, 140

2. 315, 320, 325, ◯

3. 223, 226, ☐ , 232, ☐

4. ◯ , 565, 570, ◯ , 580

5. 626, 628, 630, △ , △

6. 450, 460, ☐ , ☐ , 490

7. 782, 784, △ , △ , 790

8. 803, 806, ☐ , ☐ , ☐

Write each rule

☐ _____

◯ _____

☐ _____

△ _____

CHALLENGE

If you start at 0, can you count by 4s to exactly 100?
Why or why not?

Patterns with Numbers

. Colour the even numbers green. This is an even number pattern.

a. Give the pattern another name.

_____

b. Colour the odd numbers pink.

_____

c. What does the square look like now?

_____

411	412	413	414	415
416	416	417	418	418
419	420	421	422	423
424	425	426	427	428
429	430	431	432	433

601	602	603	604	605
606	607	608	609	610
611				
			☆	

2. Write the numbers in the green boxes.

a. Which number is above the star?

_____

b. Which number is to the left of the star?

_____

d. What is the last number in the table?

_____

e. Describe the pattern in the last column.

_____

Skip Counting

Read

Polly and Sam are having a snowball fight with their neighbours. Polly can make 20 snowballs from one bucket. Sam can throw 5 snowballs every minute.

Skip count to solve each problem.

1. Polly has 4 buckets of snow. How many snowballs can she make?

    5, 10, 15, 20, 25, 30, 35, 40, 45, 50, 55, 60, 65, 70, 75, 80

    1st bucket   2nd bucket   3rd bucket   4th bucket

2. How many snowballs can Sam throw in 3 minutes?

    _____

3. Polly makes a total of 100 snowballs. How many buckets of snow did she scoop?

    _____

4. How many buckets of snow would Polly need to make 200 snowballs?

    _____

5. How long will it take Sam to throw 200 snowballs?

    _____

Tickle Your Brain!

Solve these Math puzzles and tickle your brain.

Draw a line across (---------------), up or down (I) or diagonally (X) to make 8 3-digit numbers.

Write the numbers in order from least to greatest.

_____

_____

3	1	2
4	0	5
9	6	8

Tell how you would use skip counting to find the number of:

	Fingers on 8 hands
	Tyres in 7 bicycles
	Sides on 5 triangles
	Toes on 7 people

Complete the chart.

345	
1. One less	
2. One hundred more	
3. Ten more	
4. One hundred less	

Fun with 3-digit Numbers

Look at the number cards.

1. Choose 3 cards and write:

   a. The largest number _____

   b. The smallest number _____

   c. An even number _____

   d. An odd number _____

   e. A number less than 780 _____

   f. A number more than 450 _____

2. a. Using the cards, write 5 different 3-digit numbers.

   _____

   b. Write the numbers from smallest to greatest.

   _____

3. Use the cards to write a number:

   a. Smaller than 245.   _____

   b. Greater than 562.   _____

   c. Between 510 and 570.   _____

   d. Two even numbers less than 732.   _____

   e. Two odd numbers more than 471.   _____

CHALLENGE

Which numbers from 100–500 read the same from left to right and right to left?

Rounding Off Numbers

When we round off a number, we make it simpler by keeping its value close to the tens, hundreds or a higher place value.

For example: 17 can be rounded up to 20 and 23 can be rounded down to 20.

5+

How to round off a number to the nearest 10?

- If the number you are rounding off has 5, 6, 7, 8 or 9, in the ones place, round the number up.

Example: 28 rounded off to the nearest 10 is 30.

- If the number you are rounding off has 0, 1, 2, 3 or 4 in the ones place, round the number down.

Example: 33 rounded off to the nearest 10 is 30.

UNDER 5

Less than 5	More than 5
0 1 2 3 4	5 6 7 8 9
0	1

Rounding down ←——→ Rounding up

CHALLENGE

To what number will you round off 98?

Will it be rounding off to the nearest 10 or 100?

Round Off to Nearest 10

The kids are playing with marbles. Round off each number they scored to the nearest 10.

Round	John	Kate	Neo
Round 1	9 ⟶	34 ⟶	12 ⟶
Round 2	18 ⟶	6 ⟶	22 ⟶
Round 3	11 ⟶	20 ⟶	31 ⟶
Round 4	5 ⟶	19 ⟶	16 ⟶
Round 5	18 ⟶	39 ⟶	27 ⟶

Add the scores in each round and write the total. Round off to the nearest 10.

_____

Round Off to Nearest 100

When rounding off to the nearest 100, look at the TENS DIGIT of the number.

- If that digit is 0, 1, 2, 3 or 4, round down to the previous 100.
- If that digit is 5, 6, 7, 8 or 9, round up to the next 100.

4**2**8 ≈ ?	7**7**1 ≈ ?	9**5**7 ≈ ?
The tens digit is 2, so round down:	The tens digit is 7, so round up:	The tens digit is 5, so round up:
428 ≈ 400	771 ≈ 800	957 ≈ 1000

Round off these numbers to the nearest 100.

1.

616 ≈ _____

327 ≈ _____

2.

926 ≈ _____

560 ≈ _____

3.

470 ≈ _____

867 ≈ _____

4.

154 ≈ _____

648 ≈ _____

CHALLENGE

Whether you round up or down, the tens and ones digits change to zeros. True or false?

Rounding Off

Draw a ◯ around the number in each row that matches the description.

1.	rounds off to 30	23	37	34
2.	rounds off to 400	377	314	457
3.	rounds off to 80	85	72	83
4.	rounds off to 700	763	722	795
5.	rounds off to 50	57	48	59
6.	rounds off to 800	891	819	711
7.	rounds off to 60	56	67	69
8.	rounds off to 200	287	205	263
9.	rounds off to 300	346	368	351
10.	rounds off to 90	99	89	98

CHALLENGE

Find and tick any 3 numbers on the page that round off to 70.

Ordinal Numbers

Ordinal numbers tell us the position of an object in a series.

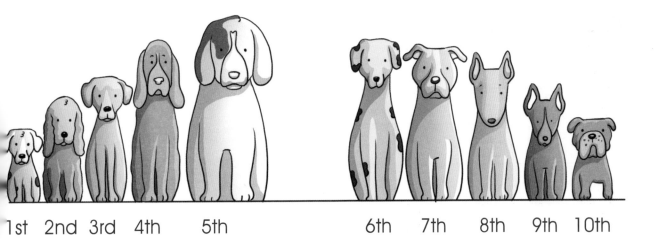

1st   2nd   3rd   4th   5th   6th   7th   8th   9th   10th

We further write ordinal numbers in this way:

21st   – twenty first

34th   – thirty fourth

56th   – fifty sixth

63rd   – sixty third

78th   – seventy eighth

80th   – eightieth

82nd   – eighty second

99th   – ninety ninth

100th   – hundredth

116th   – hundred and sixteenth

230th   – two hundred and thirtieth

Ordinal Numbers

Study the picture of the building. Answer the questions.

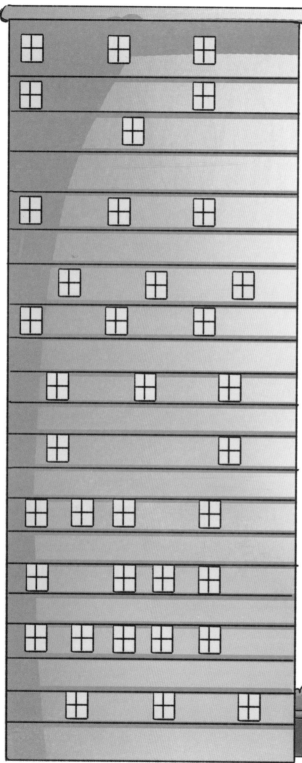

1. If the bottom floor is the 1st floor, what is the top floor?

   _____

2. How many floors have 4 windows?

   _____

3. Which floors have 5 windows?

   _____

4. How many floors are between 4th and 14th floor?

   _____

5. How many floors are above 8th floor?

   _____

6. What is the total number of floors in the building?

   _____

Ordinal Numbers

Read each problem and guess the position of animals.

Write their names in the correct order.

Zebra is third. Giraffe is last. Hippo is second. Gorilla is in front of Hippo and Seal stands after Zebra.

_____

Giraffe is second. Gorilla is fifth. Seal comes before Gorilla. Zebra is in front of Giraffe. Hippo comes after Giraffe.

_____

• Monkey is fourth. Elephant is second. Gorilla comes after Monkey. Hippo comes before. Elephant Giraffe stands before Monkey.

_____

• Wolf is third. Fox is first. Rhino is fifth. Zebra is in front of Rhino. Kangaroo is behind Fox.

_____

Ordinal Numbers

Colour first, third, sixth and seventh rectangle

Colour second, third, fifth and ninth circle

Colour second, fourth, sixth, eighth and tenth triangle

Colour first, third, sixth and seventh square

GRADE 2: FUNDAMENTAL MATHS

MATHEMATICAL OPERATIONS

Addition

Addition is putting numbers together.

The numbers that we add are called **addends**.

The result of addition is called the **sum**.

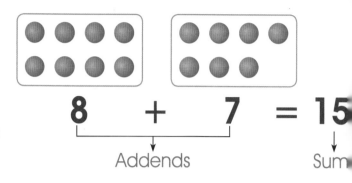

8 + 7 = 15

Addends   Sum

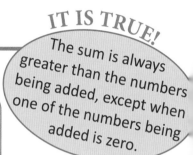

Find the sum of the following.

IT IS TRUE!
The sum is always greater than the numbers being added, except when one of the numbers being added is zero.

a.	9 + 8 =	
b.	7 + 5 =	
c.	8 + 9 + 3 =	
d.	5 + 8 + 7 =	
e.	7 + 9 =	
f.	8 + 4 =	
g.	9 + 5 + 6 =	
h.	4 + 3 + 5 =	
i.	5 + 3 + 6 =	
j.	2 + 5 + 9 =	

k.	5 + 5 =	
l.	6 + 7 =	
m.	5 + 4 + 1 =	
n.	8 + 1 + 1 =	
o.	4 + 8 + 3 =	
p.	5 + 4 =	
q.	2 + 9 + 1 =	
r.	3 + 6 + 2 =	
s.	6 + 7 + 3 =	
t.	9 + 1 + 7 =	

Challenge

Write addition sums of any 3 numbers such that they add up to 18.
How many such sums did you find?

Adding Tens and Ones

. Add the ones

	Tens	Ones
	3	8
+	4	1
		9

2. Add the tens

	Tens	Ones
	3	8
+	4	1
	7	9

IT IS TRUE!
Any number +1 = next number

dd the ones. Then add the tens.

a.
T	O
2	5
+	4

b.
T	O
3	7
+ 2	2

c.
T	O
7	1
+ 1	8

d.
T	O
4	3
+	2

e.
T	O
2	2
+ 3	7

f.
T	O
4	1
+ 2	5

g.
T	O
5	3
+ 2	4

h.
T	O
4	1
+ 2	2

i.
T	O
2	2
+ 4	3
+ 3	2

j.
T	O
6	2
+ 2	2
+ 1	4

k.
T	O
4	2
+ 2	3
+ 1	3

l.
T	O
3	4
+ 2	2
+ 2	2

Challenge

In the addition statement below, replace the numbers at ones and tens place with another numbers such that the sum is 75.

31 + 24 _____

Adding Tens and Ones with Regrouping

1. Write the numbers in **expanded form.**

2. **Add** the **tens** and **ones.**

3. **Regroup** the ones.

    6 tens and | 10 ones + 4 ones |

4. **10 ones = 1 ten,** so **carry over** 1 ten to 6 tens
    and **add**

    = 7 tens and 4 ones = 74.

Tens Ones

2 8 ⟶ 2 tens and 8 ones

+ 4 6 ⟶ 4 tens and 6 ones

6 tens and 14 one

①
   2 8
+ 4 6
─────
   7 4

Write the numbers in expanded form. Then add by regrouping.

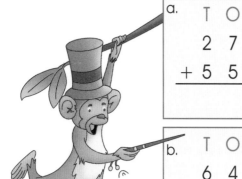

a.
    T O
    2 7
+ 5 5

27 = 2 tens and 7 ones
55 =

b.
    T O
    6 4
+ 3 8

b.
    T O
    7 2
+ 4 9

b.
    T O
    1 9
+ 2 3

Speedy Sums

Add across and down in just 4 minutes! Then write your answers in the grid.

Across

1) 14+4 3) 53+3 5) 15+3 8) 71+5
10) 42+7 12) 63+4 14) 12+4 16) 32+7
17) 30+5 19) 81+3 23) 31+6 25) 22+2
27) 23+2 29) 54+5 30) 11+6

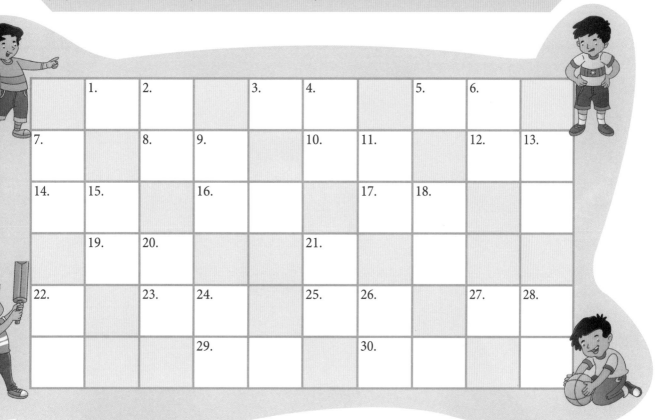

Down

2) 83+4 4) 62+2 6) 81+5 7) 30+1
9) 61+2 11) 90+3 13) 71+1 15) 62+2
18) 56+3 20) 42+1 21) 90+2 22) 63+2
24) 72+3 26) 40+1 28) 55+2

How many could you attempt?

Adding Tens and Ones with Regrouping

Short form to regroup and add

1. Add the ones.

2. Add the tens.

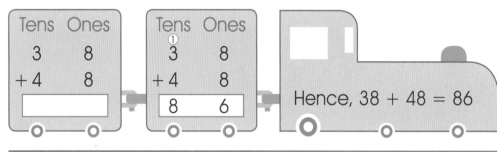

Tens	Ones
3	8
+ 4	8

Tens	Ones
① 3	8
+ 4	8
8	6

Hence, 38 + 48 = 86

Add. Regroup as needed.

a.
T	O
7	2
+ 2	9

b.
T	O
3	7
+ 4	7

c.
T	O
1	4
+ 4	8

d.
T	O
2	6
+ 3	9

e.
T	O
3	6
+ 4	4

f.
T	O
3	8
+ 3	7

g.
T	O
4	6
+ 5	9

h.
T	O
6	6
+ 6	7

i.
T	O
5	2
+ 2	9

j.
T	O
2	3
+ 3	8

k.
T	O
4	9
+ 5	5

l.
T	O
3	7
+ 9	3

Challenge

If you have 18 bananas and your mother gave two dozens more. How many bananas do you have in all now?

GRADE 2: MATHEMATICAL OPERATIONS

Adding Hundreds, Tens and Ones

. Add the ones.

	Hundreds	Tens	Ones
	1	2	6
+	3	2	2
			8

2. Add the tens.

	Hundreds	Tens	Ones
	1	2	6
+	3	2	2
		4	8

3. Add the hundreds.

	Hundreds	Tens	Ones
	1	2	6
+	3	2	2
	4	4	8

ind the sum and decode the name of a cartoon.

IT IS TRUE!
A change in the order of addends does not change the sum.
$112 + 214 = 214 + 112 = 326$

a.
```
  5 3 2
+ 1 0 6
```

b.
```
  4 2 4
+ 1 6 1
```

c.
```
  3 5 9
+ 2 2 0
```

d.
```
  7 1 4
+ 2 1 3
```

e.
```
  8 4 8
+ 1 0 1
```

f.
```
  2 3 3
+ 2 3 3
```

g.
```
  1 5 2
+ 3 4 6
```

h.
```
  6 3 1
+ 2 5 3
```

i.
```
  2 0 6
+ 5 2 3
+ 1 6 0
```

j.
```
  2 1 3
+ 4 7 0
+ 3 0 5
```

k.
```
  7 1 4
+ 1 3 1
  1 2 3
```

l.
```
  3 5 6
+   3 3
  1 0 0
```

The key!

638= E

585=C

579=Y

927=H

949=K

466=U

498=M

884=S

889=O

988=E

Challenge

The name of the cartoon is

Adding Hundreds, Tens and Ones with Regrouping

1. Add the ones and regroup.

   $9 + 4 = 13$ ones $= 1$ ten $+ 3$ ones

   Write 3 at the ones place and

   carry over 1 ten to the tens column.

	H	T	O
		①	
	4	2	9
+	2	8	4
			3

2. Add the tens.

   $1 + 2 + 8 = 11$ tens $= 1$ hundred and 1 ten

   Write 1 at the tens place and carry over

   1 hundred to the hundreds column.

	H	T	O
	①	①	
	4	2	9
+	2	8	4
		1	3

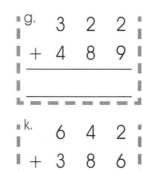

3. Add the hundreds.

   $1 + 4 + 2 = 7$ hundreds

   The sum of 429 and 284 is 713.

	H	T	O
	①	①	
	4	2	9
+	2	8	4
	7	1	3

Add. Regroup as needed

a.
```
    7 3 7
  + 4 8 9
  -------
```

b.
```
    1 3 5
  + 6 6 9
  -------
```

c.
```
    4 2 3
  + 3 2 9
  -------
```

d.
```
    9 0 5
  + 4 9 6
  -------
```

e.
```
    2 3 5
  + 4 4 6
  -------
```

f.
```
    7 4 3
  + 8 4 4
  -------
```

g.
```
    3 2 2
  + 4 8 9
  -------
```

h.
```
    1 4 8
  + 2 2 7
  -------
```

i.
```
    5 5 2
  + 2 9 9
  -------
```

j.
```
    6 6 8
  + 2 8 3
  -------
```

k.
```
    6 4 2
  + 3 8 6
  -------
```

l.
```
    7 2 7
  + 4 9 9
  -------
```

IT IS TRUE!

Always arrange the numbers according to their place value.

```
H T O          H T O
2 9 8          2 9 8
+ 4 5   ✗   +     4 5   ✓
```

Mystery Addition

Find the answer to each of the addition problems in the top square. Write your answer in the middle square. Write the letter that matches the answer in the bottom square.

598	305	317	425	567	220	145	261	932	845	763	920	100
E	B	W	A	R	Z	K	F	V	O	Y	D	J

503	759	541	687	342	848	200	790	194	270	368	424	642
Q	N	X	I	U	P	L	S	C	G	M	T	H

a.
$$142$$
$$+226$$

b.
$$423$$
$$+175$$

c.
$$321$$
$$+246$$

d.
$$161$$
$$+406$$

e.
$$463$$
$$+300$$

f.
$$162$$
$$+32$$

g.
$$144$$
$$+498$$

h.
$$225$$
$$+342$$

i.
$$498$$
$$+189$$

j.
$$520$$
$$+270$$

k.
$$279$$
$$+145$$

l.
$$114$$
$$+254$$

m.
$$231$$
$$+194$$

n.
$$602$$
$$+188$$

Addition: Word Problems

Key words that are helpful in identification of addition problems:

Total, Sum,
Added to, Combined,
Altogether

Read and solve the word problems.

1. John has 12 vanilla ice creams
   and 13 strawberry ice creams.
   How many ice creams does
   he have in all?

Solve

$$\begin{array}{r} 12 \\ + 13 \\ \hline 25 \end{array}$$ ice creams

---

2. Basket A contains 58 apples
   and Basket B contains 42
   oranges. How many fruits are
   there in both the baskets ?

_____
_____
_____ fruits

---

3. In a train, there are 640 men
   and 310 women. How many
   passengers are there in all?

_____
_____
_____ passengers

---

4. There are 356 marbles in a box
   and 274 in another. How many
   marbles are there in all?

_____
_____
_____ marbles

Subtraction

Subtraction is taking away one number from the other.

The answer of a subtraction problem is called **difference**.

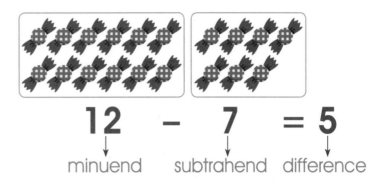

$$12 - 7 = 5$$

minuend   subtrahend   difference

Write true and false.

IT IS TRUE!
The difference between any number and zero is the number itself

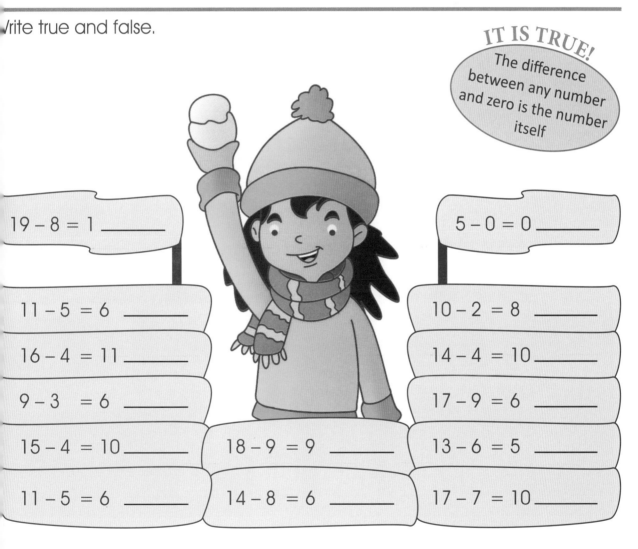

19 – 8 = 1 _____

5 – 0 = 0 _____

11 – 5 = 6 _____

10 – 2 = 8 _____

16 – 4 = 11 _____

14 – 4 = 10 _____

9 – 3 = 6 _____

17 – 9 = 6 _____

15 – 4 = 10 _____

18 – 9 = 9 _____

13 – 6 = 5 _____

11 – 5 = 6 _____

14 – 8 = 6 _____

17 – 7 = 10 _____

Challenge

Write subtraction problems of any 2 numbers such that the difference is 24.
How many such problems did you find?

Fact Family: Additon and Subtraction are Related

A fact family uses the same numbers in addition and subtraction problems.

7	3	10	10
+ 3	+ 7	− 7	− 3
10	10	3	7

a. 4
+ 7
□

b. 7
+ 4
□

c. 11
− 4
□

d. 11
− 7
□

e. 8
+ □
14

f. 6
+ 8
□

g. 14
− □
8

h. 14
− 6
□

i. 9
+ 7
□

j. □
+ 9
16

k. 16
− □
9

l. 16
− 7
□

m. 5
+ □
12

n. 5
+ 7
□

o. 12
− 7
□

p. 12
− 5
□

q. 6
+ □
15

r. 9
+ 6
□

s. 15
− 6
□

t. □
− 9
6

Challenge

Solve this. Which one number will you put in the blanks to get 15 again?

15- 4 + 2- _____ + 4- 2 + _____ = 15

Subtracting Tens and Ones

. Subtract the ones.

Tens	Ones
7	6
− 3	4
	2

2. Subtract the tens.

Tens	Ones
7	6
− 3	4
4	2

Subtract the ones and then the tens.

IT IS TRUE!
Any number − 0 = the number itself
Like 8 − 0=8

a. 4 7
  − 3 2
  ___

b. 9 6
  − 8 2
  ___

c. 6 2
  − 2 1
  ___

d. 5 1
  − 3 1
  ___

e. 6 8
  − 4 3
  ___

f. 6 9
  − 5 0
  ___

g. 5 7
  − 3 6
  ___

h. 6 6
  − 2 4
  ___

i. 8 5
  − 2 4
  ___

j. 6 3
  − 1 3
  ___

k. 9 4
  − 1 2
  ___

l. 7 2
  − 1 2
  ___

Challenge

Which is the correct form? Why?

Subtract 42 from 54.

  4 2
− 5 4
___

  5 4
− 4 2
___

GRADE 2: MATHEMATICAL OPERATIONS

Subtracting Hundreds, Tens and Ones

1. Subtract the **ones.**

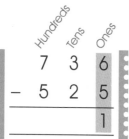

2. Subtract the **tens.**

3. Subtract the **hundred**

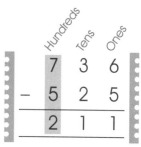

Which word would you use to describe a crane?

Find out by subtracting the ones, tens and hundreds.
Then use the letters to spell out the same.

a.

S
$$
\begin{array}{r}
8\ 2\ 3 \\
-\ 1\ 2\ 1 \\
\hline
\end{array}
$$

b.

S
$$
\begin{array}{r}
9\ 4\ 6 \\
-\ 4\ 2\ 3 \\
\hline
\end{array}
$$

c.

L
$$
\begin{array}{r}
7\ 3\ 8 \\
-\ 5\ 1\ 4 \\
\hline
\end{array}
$$

d.

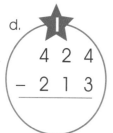

I
$$
\begin{array}{r}
4\ 2\ 4 \\
-\ 2\ 1\ 3 \\
\hline
\end{array}
$$

e.

F
$$
\begin{array}{r}
3\ 6\ 9 \\
-\ 1\ 3\ 5 \\
\hline
\end{array}
$$

f.

H
$$
\begin{array}{r}
6\ 6\ 4 \\
-\ 4\ 2\ 2 \\
\hline
\end{array}
$$

g.

G
$$
\begin{array}{r}
8\ 0\ 8 \\
-\ 6\ 0\ 5 \\
\hline
\end{array}
$$

h.

T
$$
\begin{array}{r}
9\ 1\ 3 \\
-\ 4\ 0\ 2 \\
\hline
\end{array}
$$

i.

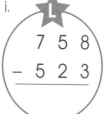

L
$$
\begin{array}{r}
7\ 5\ 8 \\
-\ 5\ 2\ 3 \\
\hline
\end{array}
$$

j.

E
$$
\begin{array}{r}
6\ 4\ 9 \\
-\ 2\ 2\ 8 \\
\hline
\end{array}
$$

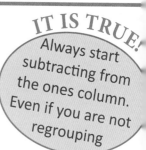

I am _____ _____ _____ _____ _____

Challenge

What is the difference between the largest 2-digit number and the smallest 3-digit even number?

_____

Subtracting Tens and Ones with Regrouping

T	O
8	3①
− 6	8

1. Subtract the ones first.
   3 − 8 can't be done.
   You need to regroup.

IT IS TRUE!
We cannot change the order of numbers and subtract. 63 − 34 (≠) 34 − 63

T	O
7̸	3̸⑬
− 6	8
	5

2. Borrow 1 ten from the tens.
   8 − 1 = 7 in the tens column.
   10 + 3 = 13 in the ones column.

T	O
8̸⑦	3̸⑬
− 6	8
1	5

3. Now subtract.
   Ones first 13 − 8 = 5
   Then the tens 7 − 0 = 7.

ill in the blanks and complete the steps.

T	O
6	3
− 3	4

1. Subtract the _____ first.
   3 − 4 can't be done.
   You need to regroup.

T	O
6⑤	3̸⑬
− 3	4
	9

2. Borrow _____ ten from the
   _____.
   _____ − 1 = 5 in the tens
   column. 10 + _____ = 13
   in the ones column.

T	O
6̸⑦	3̸⑬
− 3	4
2	9

3. Now subtract. Ones first
   _____ − 4 = _____ Then the
   tens _____ − _____ = 2.

Piling Snowballs

Help Poggy and his friend subtract the tens and ones. Be sure to regroup!

a.
```
  T O
  4 0
- 2 5
```

b.
```
  T O
  3 2
- 1 4
```

c.
```
  T O
  8 1
- 3 8
```

d.
```
  T O
  6 1
- 3 6
```

e.
```
  T O
  5 6
- 3 9
```

f.
```
  T O
  6 2
- 2 6
```

g.
```
  T O
  5 3
- 2 8
```

h.
```
  T O
  5 4
- 1 9
```

i.
```
  T O
  3 4
- 1 7
```

j.
```
  T O
  6 7
- 2 9
```

k.
```
  T O
  2 2
- 1 9
```

l.
```
  T O
  9 3
- 3 9
```

m.
```
  T O
  4 7
- 2 9
```

n.
```
  T O
  7 4
- 4 7
```

o.
```
  T O
  5 0
- 1 9
```

Challenge

Fill in circle. A, B, C and D with 2-digit numbers such that if any of two are subtracted give 24 as difference.

A D 24 B C

GRADE 2: MATHEMATICAL OPERATIONS

Subtracting Hundreds, Tens and Ones with Regrouping

. Subtract the ones first.
4 – 6 cannot be done.
Regroup 8 tens 4 ones as 7 tens and 14 ones.
14 – 6 = 8 ones

H	T	O
	7	14
6	8̸	4̸
– 3	4	6
3	3	8

. Subtract the tens. 7 – 4 = 3 tens

. Now subtract the hundreds.
6 – 3 = 3 hundreds

---

ill in the blanks and complete the steps.

9	1	4
– 4	8	6

1. Subtract the _____ first.
3-8 can't be done.
Regroup 1 ten 4 ones as _____ tens and _____ ones.

	6	3
–	3	4

2. Subtract the tens _____ can't be done.
Borrow _____ hundreds from the _____.

3. Now subtract.
Ones first _____ – 6 = _____
Then the tens _____ – _____ = 2.
At last the hundreds. _____ – _____ = _____

Fun Through Subtraction!

Subtract the ones, tens and hundreds. You must remember to regroup!

a.
H	T	O
6	5	2
− 3	8	7

b.
H	T	O
7	0	4
− 4	2	7

c.
H	T	O
6	0	5
− 4	2	6

d.
H	T	O
3	2	2
− 1	4	4

e.
H	T	O
6	3	7
− 2	4	8

f.
H	T	O
9	1	7
− 4	8	8

g.
H	T	O
4	6	5
− 3	7	7

h.
H	T	O
5	1	2
− 1	5	7

i.
H	T	O
6	2	5
− 3	7	6

j.
H	T	O
5	2	2
− 2	7	4

k.
H	T	O
8	7	2
− 2	8	4

l.
H	T	O
6	6	6
− 2	9	7

m.
H	T	O
7	5	7
− 5	6	8

n.
H	T	O
6	4	8
− 1	2	9

o.
H	T	O
5	3	4
− 3	5	6

p.
H	T	O
3	4	3
− 1	7	5

Challenge

Fill in the numbers in the squares such that it forms a subtraction statement with the numbers in the adjacent circles.

Subtraction Word Problems

ey words that are helpful in identification of subtraction problems.

how many
more, left, take away,
remaining

Read and solve the word problems.

Solve

1. Mr. Baker has 254 cupcakes. He sells 132 by evening. How many cupcakes are left with him?

$$\begin{array}{r} 254 \\ - \ 132 \\ \hline 122 \end{array}$$ cupcakes left

2. A storybook has 224 pages. Kim read only 75 pages. How many pages are left for reading?

_____
_____
_____ pages left

3. James had 425 eggs in his shop. 127 of them broke. Find the number of eggs left with him.

_____
_____
_____ eggs left

4. In a box, there are 320 red and yellow beads. If 152 beads are red, how many yellow beads does it have?

_____
_____
_____ yellow beads

5. A train was carrying 542 passengers. At a station 116 passengers got down. How many passengers were left in the train?

_____
_____
_____ passengers left

Challenge

Create your own subtraction problem using the numbers 921 and 262 and then solve it.

It's Time to Race...

Attempt these questions with your friend. Start the addition problems and your friend does the subtraction ones (or vice-versa)

The winner is the first one to correctly fill in the answers of all their problems and reach the finish line. Get, set, go!

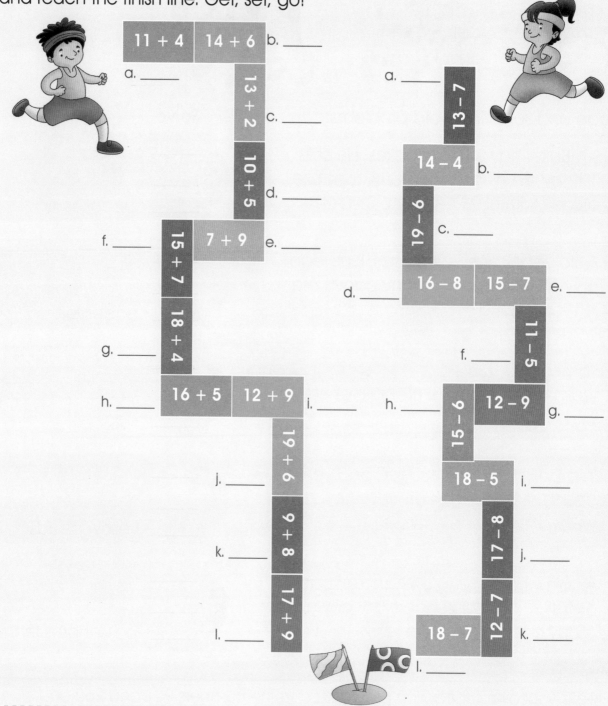

| 11 + 4 | 14 + 6 | b. _____ |

a. _____

13 + 2   c. _____

10 + 5   d. _____

f. _____   15 + 7   7 + 9   e. _____

18 + 4

g. _____

h. _____   16 + 5   12 + 9   i. _____

19 + 6

j. _____

9 + 8

k. _____

17 + 9

l. _____

a. _____   13 – 7

14 – 4   b. _____

19 – 6   c. _____

d. _____   16 – 8   15 – 7   e. _____

11 – 5

f. _____

h. _____   15 – 6   12 – 9   g. _____

18 – 5   i. _____

17 – 8   j. _____

18 – 7   12 – 7   k. _____

l. _____

FINISH

Find the Missing Digits

Find the missing digits to make the addition or subtraction problems correct.

```
   2  3  ☐
 + 4  ☐  8
 ─────────
   6  5  5
```

```
   7  ☐  7
 - 2  8  ☐
 ─────────
   ☐  9  2
```

```
   2  ☐  6
 + ☐  1  9
 ─────────
   8  0  5
```

```
   5  0  6
 - 2  9  ☐
 ─────────
   2  ☐  5
```

```
   ☐  7  7
 + 2  8  ☐
 ─────────
   9  ☐  2
```

```
   4  7  3
 - ☐  1  9
 ─────────
   2  ☐  ☐
```

```
   4  7  3
 + ☐  1  9
 ─────────
   9  ☐  2
```

```
   ☐  8  2
 - 3  ☐  8
 ─────────
   6  5  4
```

Multiplication Is Repeated Addition!

Multiplication is a different way of adding the same number again and again

The numbers that are multiplied are called **factors**

and the answer is called **product**.

X is the symbol for multiplication.

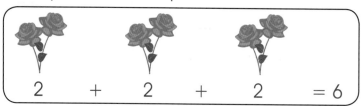

$$2 \times 3 = 6$$

factors   product

2 taken 3 times is equal to 6.
3 times 2 equal to 6.

Write each addition problem as multiplication problem. Also find the sum and product.

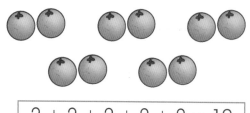

$$2 + 2 + 2 + 2 + 2 = 10$$
$$2 \times 5 = 10$$

$$\boxed{}$$

$\boxed{} \times \boxed{} = \boxed{}$

$4 + 4 = \underline{}$

$\boxed{} \times \boxed{} = \boxed{}$

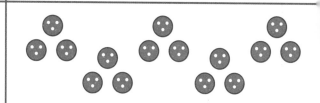

$3 + 3 + 3 + 3 + 3 = \underline{}$

$\boxed{} \times \boxed{} = \boxed{}$

Challenge

Create your own multiplication statement using any repeated addition statement.

Multiplication Statements for Arrays

Write multiplication facts for each array. The first one is done for you.

3 + 3 + 3 + 3

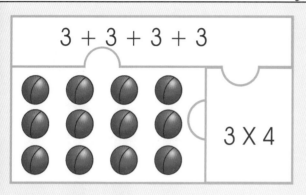

3 X 4

2 + 2

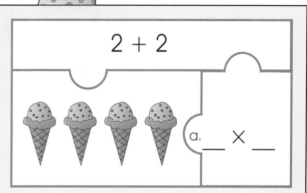

a. __ X __

4 + 4

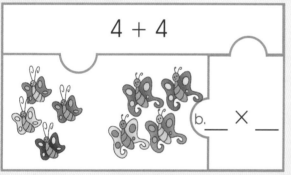

b. __ X __

8 + 8

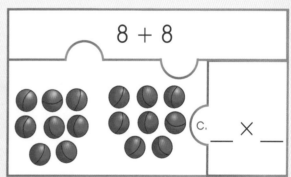

c. __ X __

5 + 5 + 5

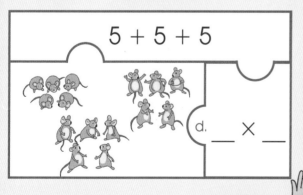

d. __ X __

6 + 6 + 6

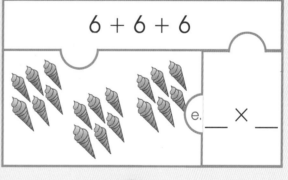

e. __ X __

Multiplication Statements for Arrays

Draw a (✓) for the multiplication statement that describes each model.

1.

a) 1 × 8   b) 4 × 8   c) 3 × 8   d) 4 × 4

2.

a) 2 × 9   b) 9 × 9   c) 3 × 9   d) 1 × 9

3.

a) 5 × 7   b) 7 × 1   c) 4 × 7   d) 6 × 7

4.

a) 1 × 8   b) 7 × 8   c) 8 × 8   d) 2 × 8

Challenge

What is the difference between the two array models?

Multiplication on the Number Line

To multiply on the number line, follow these steps:
There are two numbers while we multiply.

1) Circle the zero.
2) 1st number gives you the number of jumps.
3) 2nd number gives you the step of each jump.

$$5 \times 2 = \underline{\quad\quad}$$

Here, there are 5 jumps.
Each step is of 2 numbers.
So the product of $5 \times 2 = 10$

Find the product using the number line.

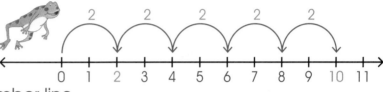

$3 \times 6 = \underline{\quad\quad}$

$4 \times 4 = \underline{\quad\quad}$

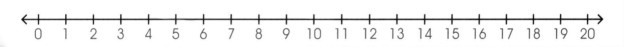

$2 \times 7 = \underline{\quad\quad}$

$5 \times 2 = \underline{\quad\quad}$

Grouping

There are 10 apples.
You can make equal groups
of 10 apples as

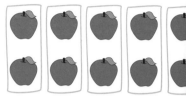

2 groups of 5 apples each   5 groups of 2 apples eac

Make groups.

There are _____ groups.

There are _____ groups.

There are _____ groups.

There are _____ groups.

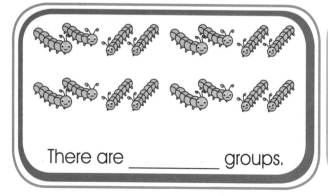

There are _____ groups.

There are _____ groups.

GRADE 2: MATHEMATICAL OPERATIONS

Division by Grouping

Division is grouping or splitting into equal parts or groups. (÷) is the symbol of division.

To write division fact:

1. Count and write the total items.
2. Then divide the items into number of groups given. Write the items in each group.
3. Count the number of groups formed.
4. The answer is the number of groups.

Divide into group of 2:

Total items	Items in each group	Number of group
8	÷ 2	= 4

Divide into groups and write division facts.

	Total items	Items in each group	Number of groups
	☐	÷ ☐	= ☐
	☐	÷ ☐	= ☐
	☐	÷ ☐	= ☐
	☐	÷ ☐	= ☐
	☐	÷ ☐	= ☐

Division Sentences

Write division sentences for these groups.

$$6 \div 2 = 3$$

$$\square \div \square = \square$$

$$\square \div \square = \square$$

$$\square \div \square = \square$$

$$\square \div \square = \square$$

$$\square \div \square = \square$$

Challenge

Four groups of 2 caps each are given here. Make them 2 groups with equal number of caps.

These Squares Are Magical!

Complete these magic squares. In each square the rows, columns and diagonals add up to the same number!

Missing Operations!

Can you find out the missing operation? Give it a try!

Only use + and − signs.

10 _____ 2 = 8   11 _____ 2 = 9

16 _____ 4 = 20   12 _____ 5 = 17

14 _____ 8 = 6   15 _____ 9 = 6

7 _____ 6 = 13   18 _____ 1 = 19

20 _____ 2 = 18   13 _____ 4 = 17

Use any combination of + and − and make a total of 12 with each of the given sets of numbers. You can use a number more than once. The first one has been done for you.

1 2 3 4   **4 + 2 + 3 + 3**

5 6 1 2

2 3 7 1

4 5 3 2

GEOMETRY AND MEASUREMENT

Identifying Plane Shapes

Identify each shape. Then write its name matching its number in the table below.

3-	4-	5-	6-
7-	8-	9-	10-

GRADE 2: GEOMETRY AND MEASUREMENT

Quadrilaterals

A quadrilateral is a closed figure with four sides and four angles.

They can be grouped by sides, angles, length and parallel sides.

Cross out the shapes that are not quadrilaterals. Then write the correct name for each quadrilateral.

 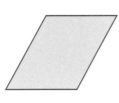  

_____ _____ _____ _____

  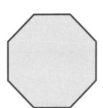 

_____ _____ _____ _____

CHALLENGE

Fill in the table to compare the quadrilaterals.

Figure	Number of sides	Parallel sides	Angles
Square	4 equal sides	2 pairs of parallel sides	4 right angles

Properties of Quadrilaterals

Read each definition below. Inside each quadrilateral, write the number of the definition that matches it.

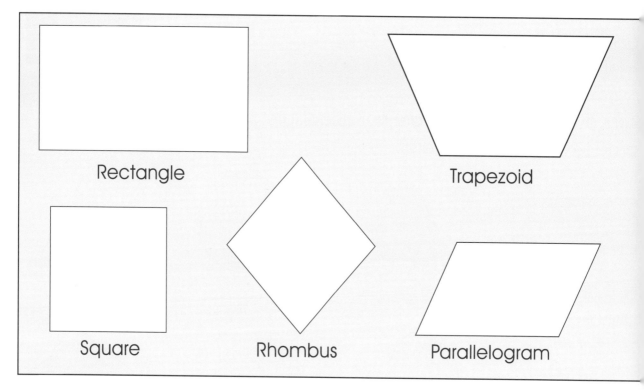

Definitions

1. a four-sided figure with all sides equal
2. a four-sided figure with opposite sides equal and parallel
3. a four-sided figure with only one set of parallel sides
4. a figure with all angles equal to 90° and all sides equal
5. a figure with opposite sides parallel but angles may vary

CHALLENGE

Tick the statements that are true.

1. A parallelogram is a kind of rectangle.
2. A square and rhombus are similar.
3. A rhombus is similar to a parallelogram.

Congruent Figures

Two figures are congruent if they are exactly the same shape and size. Their corresponding sides and angles are equal.

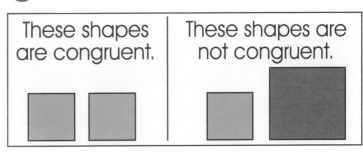

These shapes are congruent.	These shapes are not congruent.

In each row, tick the shape that is congruent to the first one.

   a.   b.   c.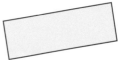

   a.    b.   c.

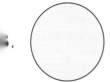   a.   b.   c.

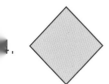   a.   b.   c.

   a.    b.    c.

QUICK TIP

Congruent shapes may appear different because one is shifted or rotated a certain way, but they're still the same shape. All the sides of one shape are the same length as the corresponding sides of the other.

Congruent Figures

Identify the congruent figures for each shape from the picture given below. Write the matching letters.
Not all shapes may have congruent pairs.

1.  _ _ _ _

2.  _ _ _ _

3.  _ _ _ _

4.  _ _ _ _

5.  _ _ _ _

6.  _ _ _ _

7.  _ _ _ _

8.  _ _ _ _

9.  _ _ _ _

10.  _ _ _ _

11.  _ _ _ _

12.  _ _ _ _

CHALLENGE

Why are these pairs not congruent? Explain.

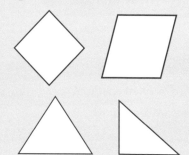

Congruent Shapes

Use a pencil and a ruler to draw a congruent shape for each figure on the grid. Colour when you draw.

A.

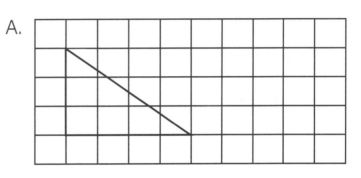

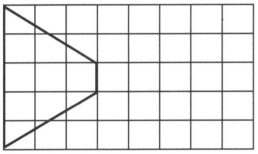

C.

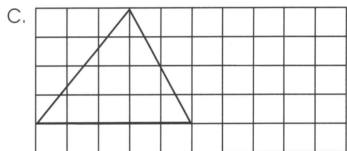

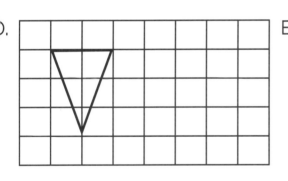

E.

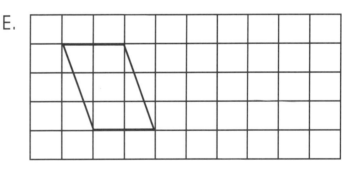

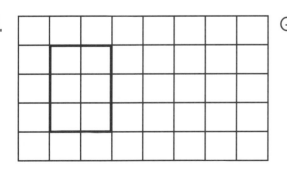

G.

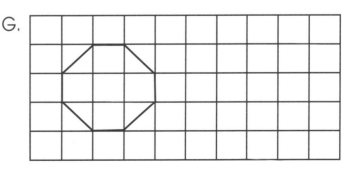

Solid Shapes

Tick the solid shape that matches each statement.

I am without any corners.

I am without any corners.

All my faces except one are triangles.

I have faces that are all squares.

My flat face is a circle.

I have 8 corners with all my faces rectangles.

GRADE 2: GEOMETRY AND MEASUREMENT

Solid Figures

Look at each model. Write the shape of each model and complete the table.

1.

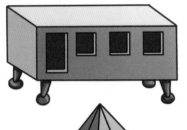

2.

3.

4.

5.

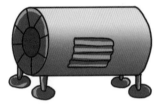

6.

Shape of the model	Number of faces	Number of edges	Number of corners
1.			
2.			
3.			
4.			
5.			
6.			

CHALLENGE

Each model is made up of 2 solid shapes. Identify and name them.

Word bank

Cone

Pyramid

Sphere

Cylinder

Cube

Rectangular prism

Solid Shapes

Each side of a solid figure is a face. For example:

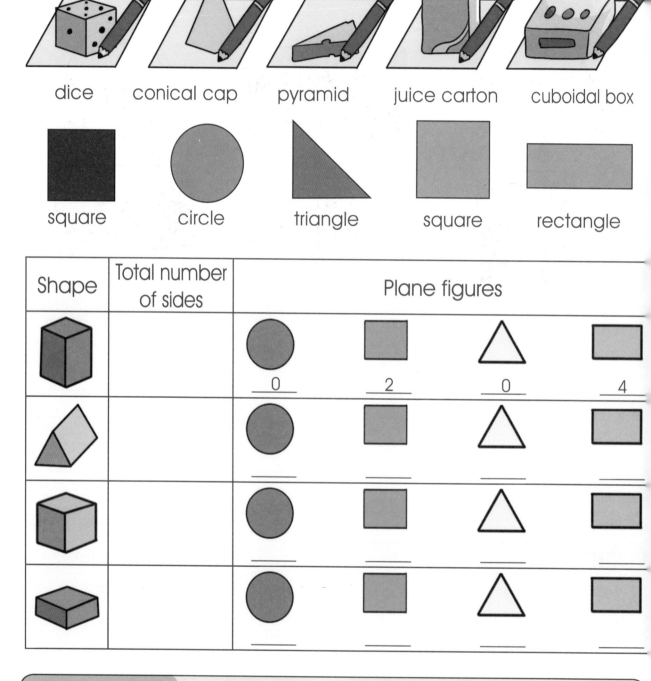

Shape	Total number of sides	Plane figures			
		○ __0__	■ __2__	△ __0__	▭ __4__
		○ ____	■ ____	△ ____	▭ ____
		○ ____	■ ____	△ ____	▭ ____
		○ ____	■ ____	△ ____	▭ ____

CHALLENGE

Draw the top view of a cube, a cone and a rectangular prism. How do they look like?

Attributes of Solid Figures

Which shape would you add to each shape below to form a new shape? Draw it.

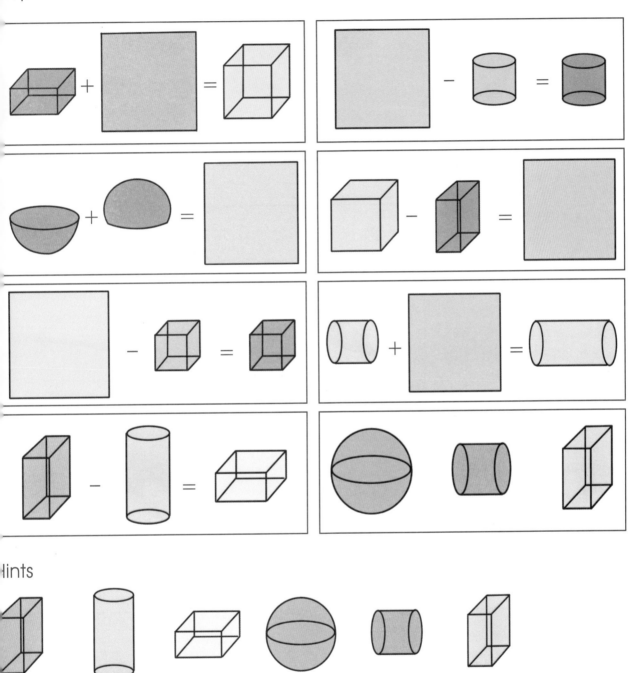

Hints

CHALLENGE

How would the number of faces and edges change when you join two cubes side by side?

Flip, Turn and Slide

Slide	Flip	Turn

Move an item in any direction without rotating it	To turn over or reflect	To rotate or turn around

Write flip, slide or turn for each.

1. 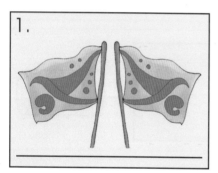	2. 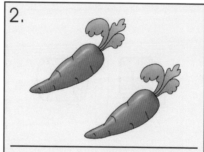	3. 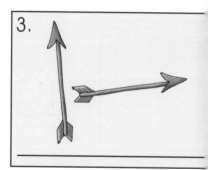
_____	_____	_____

4. 	5. 	6. 
_____	_____	_____

TRY IT

Draw a letter to show flip and slide.

L   M

Flip, Turn and Slide

Draw a circle around the objects to show flip, slide and turn using the colour code.

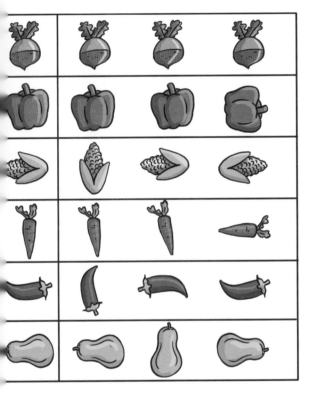

flip = yellow
slide = green
turn = blue

CHALLENGE

Draw a leaf. Then draw and label its flip, slide and turn.

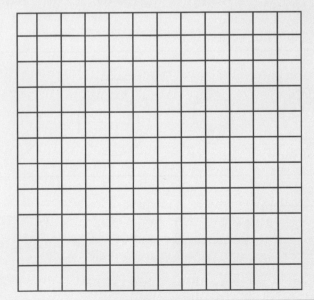

Flip, Turn and Slide

Look at the figures below. Tick the one that is congruent to the first one in each row. Then label it as flip, slide or turn.

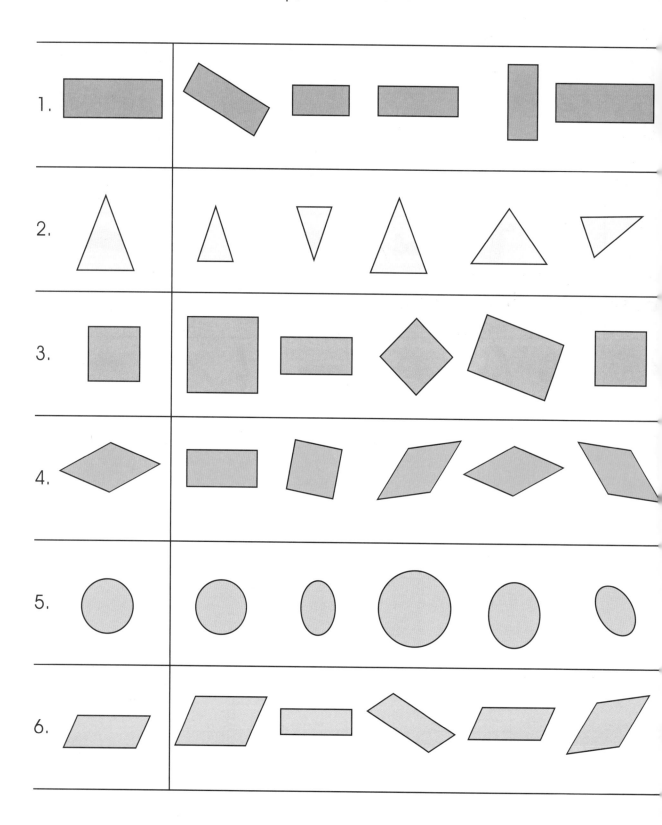

Equal Parts

onny has painted all the shapes. Draw a circle
round the shapes that are divided into equal
arts.

A shape can be divided into two, three, four or many equal parts.

Fractions

Look at the shapes. Each shape is divided into different number of equal parts.

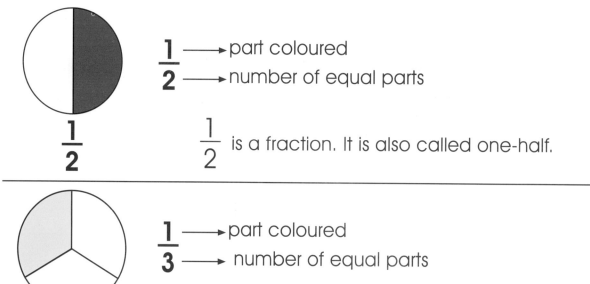

$\dfrac{1}{2}$ ⟶ part coloured

$\dfrac{1}{2}$ ⟶ number of equal parts

$\dfrac{1}{2}$ is a fraction. It is also called one-half.

$\dfrac{1}{3}$ ⟶ part coloured

$\dfrac{1}{3}$ ⟶ number of equal parts

$\dfrac{1}{3}$ is a fraction. It is also called one-third.

$\dfrac{1}{4}$ ⟶ part coloured

$\dfrac{1}{4}$ ⟶ number of equal parts

$\dfrac{1}{4}$ is a fraction. It is also called one-fourth or quarter.

A fraction also tells us that many parts of a whole are being used.

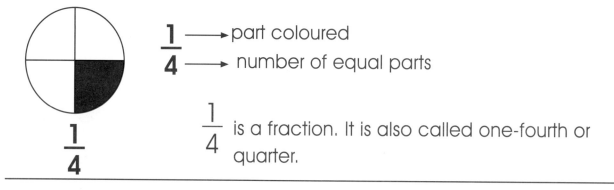
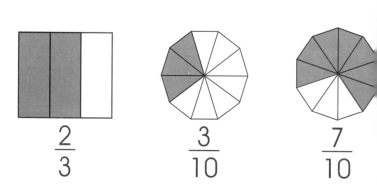

$\dfrac{2}{3}$ $\qquad$ $\dfrac{3}{10}$ $\qquad$ $\dfrac{7}{10}$

Fractions

Write the fraction for the shaded part.

Fractions

Shade each shape to show the fraction. Then write the fraction for the unshaded part.

A. shaded = $\frac{3}{4}$ unshaded =	B. shaded = $\frac{1}{2}$ unshaded =	C. shaded = $\frac{2}{4}$ unshaded =	D. shaded = $\frac{5}{6}$ unshaded =
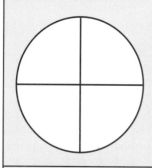	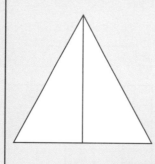		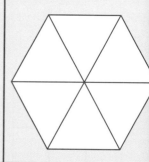
E. shaded = $\frac{2}{3}$ unshaded =	F. shaded = $\frac{3}{10}$ unshaded =	G. shaded = $\frac{2}{6}$ unshaded =	H. shaded = $\frac{4}{6}$ unshaded =
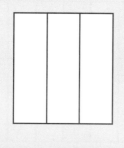	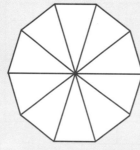	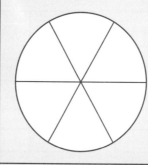	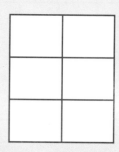
I. shaded = $\frac{7}{8}$ unshaded =	J. shaded = $\frac{1}{4}$ unshaded =	K. shaded = $\frac{1}{2}$ unshaded =	L. shaded = $\frac{4}{8}$ unshaded =
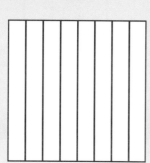	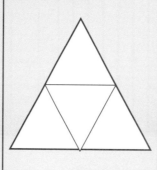	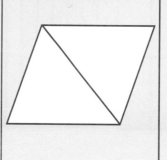	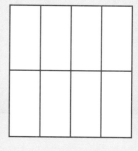

GRADE 2: GEOMETRY AND MEASUREMENT

Telling Time to the Hour and Half Hour

Look at the small hand. The number it points is the hour. Look at the big hand. If it is at 12, write **o'clock**.

Look at the last number the hour hand passed. Do not pass the hour hand. Look at the big hand. If it is at 6, write **30 minutes or half past**.

Write the time below each clock.

1

_____

2

_____

3

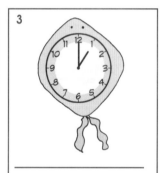

_____

4

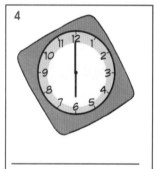

_____

5

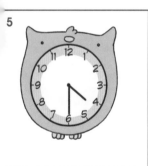

_____

6

_____

7

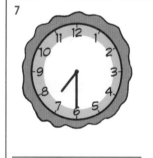

_____

8

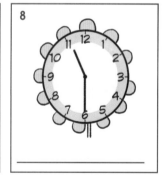

_____

9

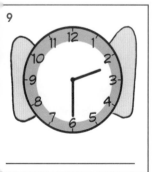

_____

10

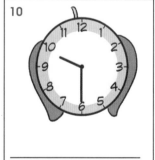

_____

11

_____

12

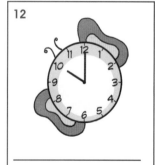

_____

Telling Time to Quarter Hour

 When the minute hand is at 3, we write **quarter past.**

 When the minute hand is at 9, we write **quarter to.**

Write the time on the lines below each clock.

1
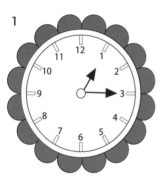
_____

2
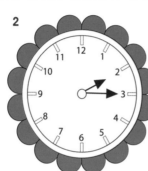
_____

3
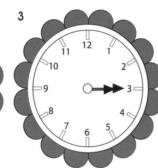
_____

4
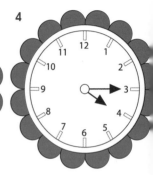
_____

5

_____

6
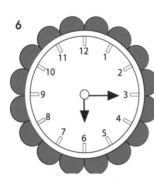
_____

7
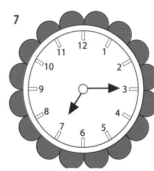
_____

8
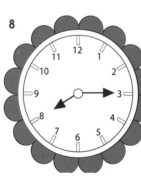
_____

9
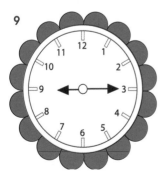
_____

10
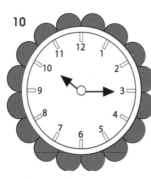
_____

11
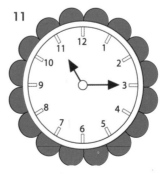
_____

12
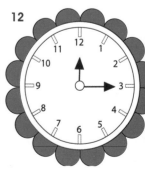
_____

GRADE 2: GEOMETRY AND MEASUREMENT

Telling Time

Identify the time on each clock. Then draw the symbol matching the correct clock.

[ ] 3:00

[ ] 6:15

[ ] 2:45

[ ] 9:30

[ ] 5:30

[ ] 11:15

[ ] 1:45

[ ] 12:15

[ ] quarter to two

[ ] half past five

[ ] three o'clock

[ ] quarter after twelve

[ ] half past nine

[ ] quarter after six

[ ] quarter to three

[ ] quarter after eleven

Telling Time to Minutes

What time is it? Draw the hands.

Look at the hour hand, what it's passed and STOP!

5 minutes

Look at the minute hand. Start at 12 and count by 5s!

1

| 4 : 00 |

It's four o'clock.

2

| : |

It's quarter past five.

3

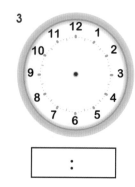

| : |

It's half past nine.

4

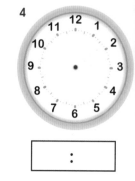

| : |

It's eight o'clock

5

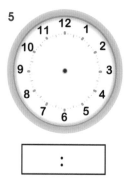

| : |

It's five minutes after three.

6

| : |

It's ten minutes to four.

7

| : |

It's twenty minutes to seven.

8

| : |

It's ten minutes after six.

204

Measuring Length in Centimetres

Length is how long or far something is. We measure length in centimetres, inches or metres.

cm= centimetres, in= inches, m= metres

centimetre
The length of a paper clip

inch
The length of a pinky finger

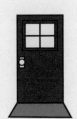
metres
a bit more than width of a door

Look at each fence. Guess the length and then use a ruler to measure actually.

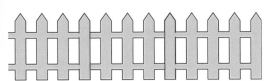

guess = _____ cm

actual measure = _____ cm

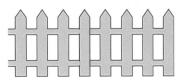

guess = _____ cm

actual measure = _____ cm

guess = _____ cm

actual measure = _____ cm

guess = _____ cm

actual measure = _____ cm

guess = _____ cm

actual measure = _____ cm

guess = _____ cm

actual measure = _____ cm

CHALLENGE

Draw a fence that is longer than the longest fence on this page.

Measuring Length in Centimetres

Use a ruler to measure these lines in centimetres. Then add all the measurements and write the total.

Total length = _____ cm

Total length = _____ cm

Total length = _____ cm

Guess the length of each object in centimetres. Then measure to find the length.

Objects to measure	My guess	Actual measurement	Colour a star for each correct guess
My hand	_____ cm	_____ cm	☆
My book	_____ cm	_____ cm	☆
A pencil	_____ cm	_____ cm	☆
My foot	_____ cm	_____ cm	☆

GRADE 2: GEOMETRY AND MEASUREMENT

Measuring Length in Inches

ow long are these things? Measure in inches and write.

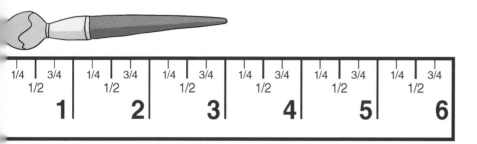

_____

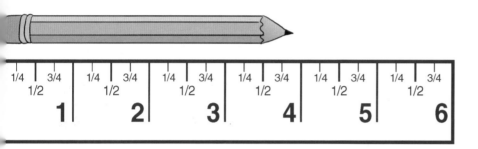

_____

Guess the length of each object in inches. Then measure to find the
ength.

Objects to measure	My guess	Actual measurement	Colour a star for each correct guess
My hand	_____ in	_____ in	☆
My book	_____ in	_____ in	☆
A pencil	_____ in	_____ in	☆
My foot	_____ in	_____ in	☆

CHALLENGE

How could you measure the length of this line?

 How long is it?

Weight

Weight is how heavy or light something is. We measure weight in grams and kilograms.

kg= kilograms   g= grams

Envelope **measured in Grams**

Rock **measured in kilograms**

Measure the weight of each object and write it below.

1
_____ kg

2
_____ g

3
_____ kg

4
_____ kg

5
_____ kg

6
_____ kg

7
_____ g

8
_____ kg

Weight

Draw a pointer on each scale to show the weight of each object below.

2 kg	7.5 kg	4.75 kg	8 kg
3.4 kg	1.5 kg	9.5 kg	5.5 kg

1 kg

CHALLENGE

Can you find something that is of the same weight as you are.

Weight

Calculate the unknown weight to balance each scale.

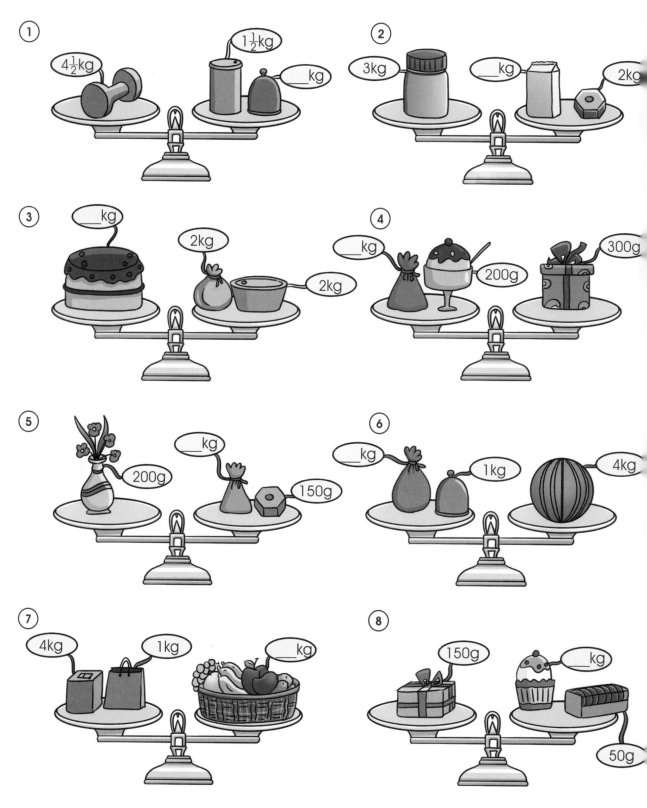

① $4\frac{1}{2}$kg $1\frac{1}{2}$kg   ___kg

② 3kg   ___kg   2kg

③ ___kg   2kg   2kg

④ ___kg   200g   300g

⑤ 200g   ___kg   150g

⑥ ___kg   1kg   4kg

⑦ 4kg   1kg   ___kg

⑧ 150g   ___kg   50g

Capacity

Capacity is how much liquid a container can hold. We measure capacity in litres and millilitres.

l= litres   **ml= millilitres**

Glass of lemonade **measured in millilitres**

oil can **measured in litres**

These containers measure millilitres.

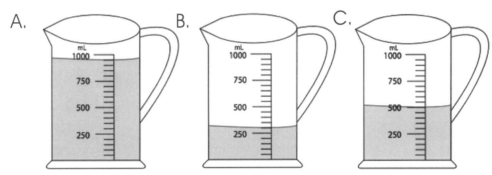

A.   B.   C.

1. How much water is in:
   Container A: _____ Container B: _____
   Container C: _____

2. How much water is more in:
   C than B ? _____ A than C? _____ A than B? _____

3. Which container has water almost equal to 1L?
   _____

4. How much must be added to container C to make it 1 L?
   _____

CHALLENGE

Take a bottle and with a marker show where you think ½ L is. Measure and check.

Fun with Measurement

Find an object 1 cm in length.	Find an object 5 cms in length.	Find an object 50 millimeters in length.
Find an object or part of the classroom that is 5 meters in length.	Find an object 12 inches in length.	Find an object 1 foot in length.
Find an object 3 feet in length.	Find an object 1 yard in length.	Find an object or part of the classroom that is 3 yards in length.
Find an object 10 cm in length.	Find an object 15 millimeters in length.	Find an object 3 inches in length.

DATA HANDLING

Favourite Fruits

Miss Lee has grown 3 types of fruits. She is making fruit salad for her nephews and nieces. They all visit her farm. This list shows the fruits the children like.

I like grapes

Shirin
Lisa
Bob
Pam
Emma
Poppy

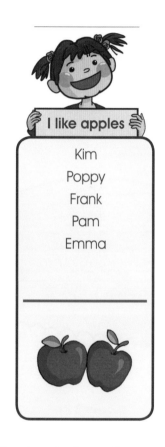

I like apples

Kim
Poppy
Frank
Pam
Emma

I like pears

Poppy
Pam
Lisa
Bob
Ronny
Shirin
Emma

1. How many children visit Miss Lee's farm?

_____

2. Name the children who like all the fruits.

_____

3. Who likes both grapes and apples?

_____

4. Who likes only pears?

_____

5. Which two fruits should Miss Lee use for the fruit salad? Why?

_____

Try this!

Which fruit do you like? Add your name to Miss Lee's list. Will this change the fruits Miss Lee would use for the fruit salad?

Favourite Pastime

eo's friends are fond of different pastimes.

Help him make a list of pastimes that are popular among his friends.
Use the information from the pictures to complete the table.

Pastime	Number of Children
skating	3

Which pastime is the most popular among Neo's friends?

_____

Tally Chart

A tally chart is made using tallies to record data or information.

Susan made a tally chart to record the favourite subjects of her classmates. Help her answer the questions by interpreting the chart.

Subject	Tally count
Math	卌 卌
Reading	卌 卌 卌 I
Science	卌 卌 卌 卌
Social Science	卌 卌 III
Writing	IIII

1. How many of Susan's classmates have Science as their favourite subject?

_____

2. How many more students like Reading than Math?

_____

3. Did more students choose Math or Social Science?

_____

4. Which subject has the most votes?

_____

5. Which subject has the least votes?

_____

Try this!

Make a tally chart to show the favourite subjects of your classmates.

Where are you placed in the tally chart?

Score High!

ive students of Grade 2 participated in the Science Quiz. They made a tally
o show the marks they had scored so far.

Student	Tally count
	卌 卌 卌 卌 卌 卌 II
Joy	卌 卌 卌 卌 III
	卌 卌 卌 卌 卌 IIII
Jill	

Kate 32 Lilly 24 Suzie 27

Joy 23 Jill 15

- Something has gone wrong with the tally chart. Correct it so that it shows all the information.

- One of the students is hoping to win the quiz. Who do you think it might be?

_____

- Write down 5 things you know from the tally chart. Take help of the hint box.

_____

_____

_____

_____

_____

Hint Box!

Number of children participated in the quiz

Who scored the highest?

Who scored the lowest?

Scored more than Joy

Scored less than Jill

On the Sea Shore!

Martha saw wonderful sea creatures when she was on a holiday. Help her make a tally chart to list the creatures.
These pictures show what she saw.

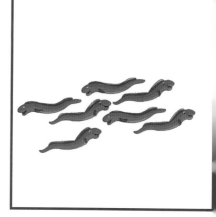
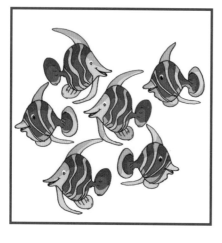
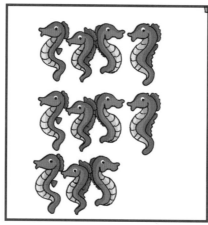

GRADE 2: DATA HANDLING

se the information on page 218 to help Martha make a tally chart.

Sea creature	Tally count

se the chart to answer these questions.

. How many of each creature did Martha see?

angelfish _____ turtle _____ shark _____
crab _____ jelly fish_____ starfish _____

. Which creature did she see the most?

_____

. How many crabs did she see more than the turtle?

_____

. How many creatures did she see in all?

_____

Try this!

Imagine you saw 2 more of each type of sea creature than Martha. How will your tally chart change? Make a new chart.

Frequency Table

The **frequency** of a data value is the number of times the data value occur. For example: If 3 students have a score of 55 in mathematics, then the scor of 55 is said to have a frequency of 3.

A **frequency table** is constructed by arranging these collected data values.

Mr. Paul has made a frequency table to show the sales of story books last week. Read the table and answer the questionnaire.

Story Book	Number of books sold
Cinderella	1000
Rapunzel	1560
Snow White and the Seven Dwarfs	2380
Beauty and the Beast	1300
Pinocchio	2000
Peter Pan	1220

1. Which is the best-selling story book?

---

2. Which book sold fewest the last week?

---

3. How many copies did Mr. Paul sell of each book? Arrange them in the order of fewest to the most.

---

4. Which book should Mr. Paul always have in stock to get good sales?

Holiday Time

nda is planning for a travel package. She made a tally chart to show
oliday bookings by different people of her city.

Country	Tally	Frequency
Italy	⊞⊞ ‖	7
Bangkok	⊞⊞ ⊞⊞ ⊞⊞	15
France	⊞⊞ ⊞⊞ ⊞⊞ ‖‖	19
Australia	⊞⊞ ‖	6
Singapore	⊞⊞ ‖‖	8

omplete the frequency table and answer the questions.

. Which was the most popular country to visit?

_____

. Which countries did more than 10 people book?

_____

. Which countries did less than 10 people book?

_____

. Linda needs to make arrangements for 3 more people in Bangkok, Italy
and Australia. What would be the number of bookings for these countries
now?

Bangkok _____

Italy _____

Australia _____

At the Store

Miss Carol recorded the number of different pieces of clothing in her store. She made some notes. Complete the frequency table for her.

Piece of clothing	Frequency

1. How many of each piece of clothing does Miss Carol have?

Trousers _____   Shirts _____   Skirts _____

Dresses _____   Shorts _____

2. How many are only for boys? _____ only for girls? _____

3. How many pieces of clothing does she have altogether?

_____

4. How did you work it out?

_____

Try this!

What will be the total number of pieces of clothing if 5 is added to each item?

Pictogram

A pictogram is a graph used to compare data using pictures or symbols.

Ben made a pictogram to record the number of little creatures in his garden. Check to see if he has got it right. Add more circles if they are needed and cross out any that are not needed.

⬤ = 1 creature

Ants	⬤ ⬤ ⬤ ⬤ ⬤ ⬤
Caterpillars	⬤ ⬤ ⬤
Butterflies	⬤ ⬤ ⬤ ⬤
Bees	⬤ ⬤ ⬤ ⬤ ⬤ ⬤
Ladybirds	⬤ ⬤ ⬤ ⬤ ⬤
Beetles	⬤ ⬤

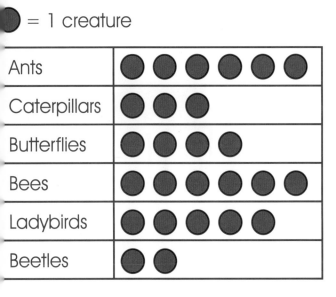

How many of each creature does Ben find?

ants _____   caterpillars _____   butterflies _____

bees _____   ladybirds _____   beetles _____

Mr Roger has collected some musical instruments for the orchestra. Look at the pictures given below.

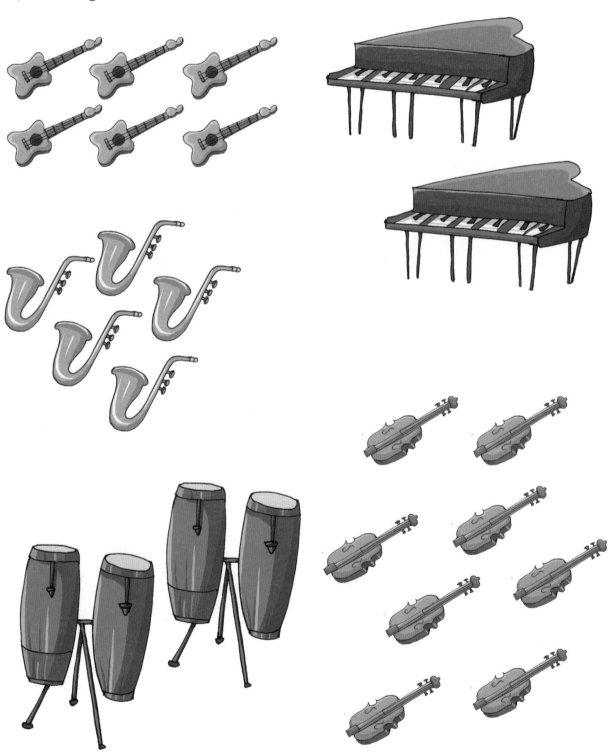

Complete the pictogram to show the different types of instruments he has collected.

▲ = 1 instrument

guitar	trumpet	piano	drum	violin

Number of Instruments (vertical axis label)

How many of each instrument does Mr Roger have?

violin _____   drum _____   guitar _____

trumpet _____   piano _____

Try this!

Make up five questions from this pictogram to ask your friend.

Christmas Presents

The students in Kelly's school voted for the present they want for Christmas. The pictogram shows what the students said.

 = 2 presents

Remote control car	Skates	Chocolates	Board game	Water colours	Soft toy	Robot

Number of gifts

1. How many of each present did the students vote for?

remote control car _____   skates _____

chocolates _____   board game _____

water colours _____   dress _____

soft toy _____   robot _____

Sorting Objects

Bob sorted objects according to their colour. Is his pictogram correct?
Correct it for him.

● = 2 objects   ◗ = 1 object

Bob's List	
Red	13
Green	16
Blue	11
Yellow	20

Bob's List	
Brown	25
White	5
Black	8
Pink	12

	●●●●●●◗
Blue	●●●●
	●●●◗
Yellow	●●●●●●●●
	●●●●●●●●●●●●●
	●●●
	●
Pink	●●●●

Try this!

Look around your room and sort different objects according to their
colour. Make a pictogram to show this.

Jam Factory

Henry's food store packs jam bottles every day. Use the information in the list and make a pictogram to show the data.

Monday	25
Tuesday	45
Wednesday	40
Thursday	30
Friday	50
Saturday	22
Sunday	15

Monday	Tuesday	Wednesday	Thursday	Friday	Saturday	Sunday

Try this!

How many bottles of jam were packed in the week? What is the easiest way to work it out?

GRADE 2: DATA HANDLING

Bar Graph

bar graph uses bars to show a picture of the data collected.

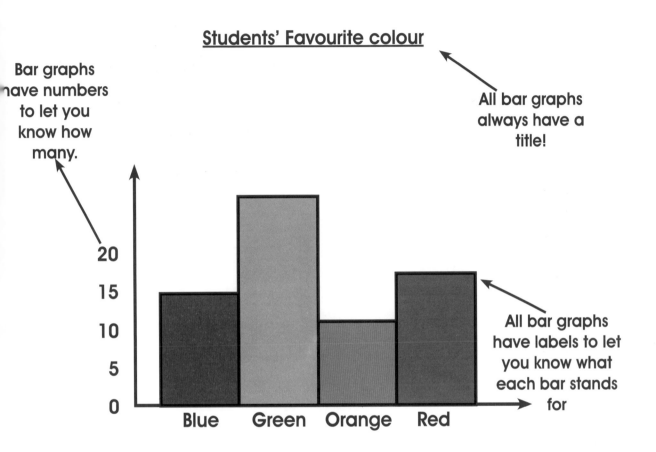

Bar graphs have numbers to let you know how many.

Students' Favourite colour

All bar graphs always have a title!

All bar graphs have labels to let you know what each bar stands for

We use a bar graph to compare data.

Steps to construct a bar graph:
- Gather data
- Write a title
- Draw a horizontal line and a vertical line
- Add numbers on vertical line
- Write labels on horizontal line
- Determine the intervals
- Draw bars to show your data

Pets at Home

Polly and her classmates have pets. The bar chart shows how many children have these pets.

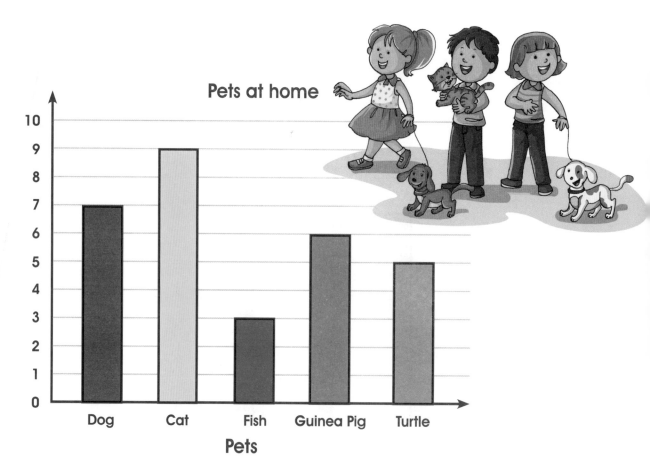

1. How many of each pet does the graph show?

   dog _____, cat _____, fish _____

   guinea pig _____, turtle _____

2. Which pet do most children have?

   _____

3. Which pet do least children have?

   _____

Puppet Show

lelly and friends want to put a puppet show. They voted which one to do.
The bar chart shows the results of the voting.

Puppet Show

Clown Pirate Sailor Prince Princess Magician

Puppet Character

. How many children voted for each puppet?

clown _____, pirate _____, sailor _____

prince _____, princess _____, magician _____

. Which puppet should the children choose?

_____

. Which puppet is not popular among the children?

_____

Temperatures in Molly's Town

The bar chart shows the average temperature of Molly's town last year. Study the graph and answer the questions.

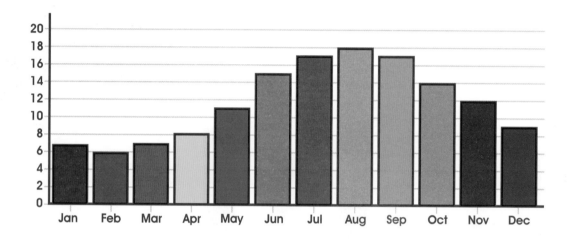

1. What is the average temperature for these months?

   January _____,   April _____,   June _____

   August _____,   October _____,   December _____

2. Which is the hottest month?

   _____

3. Which is the coldest month?

   _____

4. What is the difference between temperature of August and January?

   _____

Try this!

Which is the best month to go on a beach holiday to Molly's town?

Quick tip!

The more temperature, the hotter it is. The less temperature, the colder it is.

Creating a Bar

efore you create a bar chart, let's brainstorm
ne steps you need to follow.

ne frequency table shows favourite snacks of
eople at Mac's restaurant.

Snacks	Number of people
Burger	10
French fries	8
Noodles	6
Cheese puff	12
Corn chips	15

Jse the following to make a bar chart.

. What will your title be?

_____

2. What will you call the horizontal line?

_____

3. What labels will you use on the horizontal line?

_____

4. What will you call the vertical line?

_____

5. What numbers will you use on the vertical line?

_____

Now make a bar chart in your notebook.

Flowers in the Garden

Nora made a frequency table to show the number of flowers in her garden

Name of flower	Frequency
Rose	15
Lily	11
Tulip	9
Sunflower	12
Daisy	8
Orchid	6

Make a bar chart to show this information.

The School Library

ew books on different subjects have been added to the school library.
ook at the picture and complete the frequency table. Then draw a bar
hart on page 24 to show this data.

ubject	Number of books

Drawing

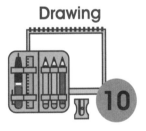 10

Physical Education

 4

Painting

 7

Creation

 8

Geometry

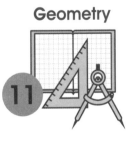 11

Geography

 5

Math

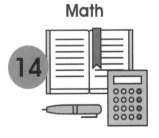 14

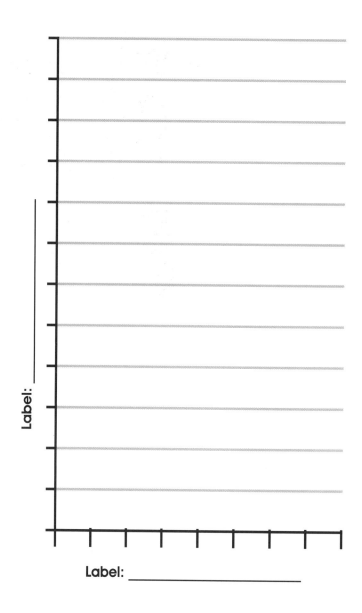

Label: _____

Label: _____

Try this!

How many new books are added to the school library altogether?

Cookies for Sale

The picture below shows the number of different cookie packets ordered at Mr. Paul's bakery.

Orange Cookies
10

Choco chip cookies
8

Strawberry Cookies
9

Salty Cookies
5

Oats Cookies
6

Cashew Cookies
15

Complete the frequency table.

Cookies	Number of boxes ordered

Try this!

Make notes from the above data that you will use to make a bar chart

Cookies for Sale

Use your frequency table on page 26 and make a bar chart.

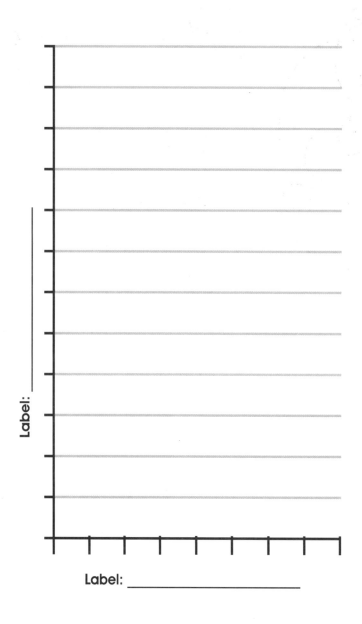

Label:

Label: _____

Venn Diagrams

A Venn diagram is a visual tool used to compare and contrast two (sometimes three) different things. A Venn diagram is made up of two large circles that intersect with each other to form a space in the middle.

Steps to make a Venn diagram

Compare- how two things are alike or same

Contrast- how two things are different

Write the numbers in 2's table here

Write the numbers in both the tables here

Write the numbers in 3's table here

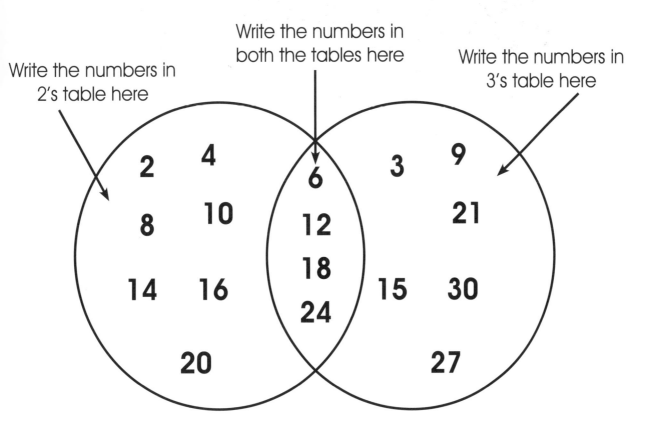

Venn diagram to compare numbers in 2's table and 3's table

Try this!

Make a Venn diagram to compare numbers in 2's table and 6's table.

Strawberry or Vanilla

Ronny asked his friends if they liked strawberry ice cream or vanilla. He recorded what they said in this Venn diagram.

1. How many of Ronny's friends like:

   Strawberry _____, Vanilla _____, both _____,

   Only strawberry _____, Only Vanilla _____

2. How many friends did Ronny ask?

_____

Try this!

Ask your friends their choice between strawberry and vanilla. Make a Venn diagram to show your results.

Amazing Animals

James studied about many animals. Help him sort the animals that live on land and in water. Help him make a Venn diagram.

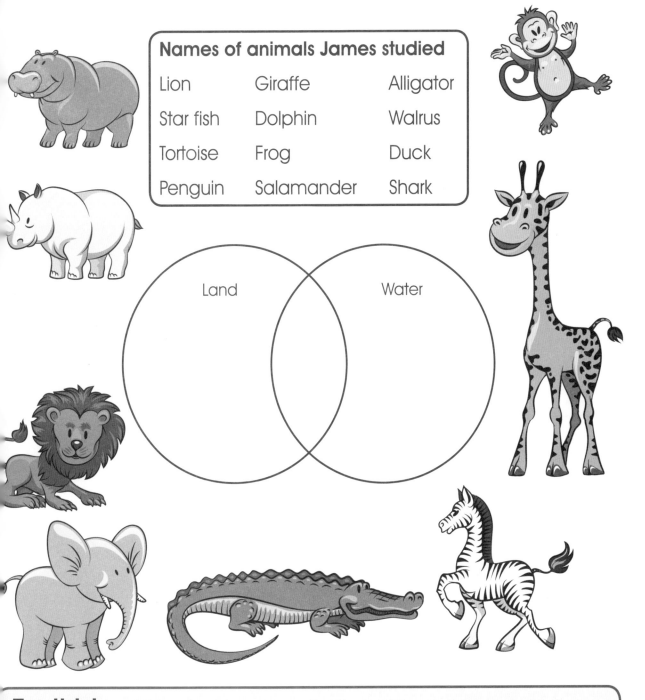

Names of animals James studied

Lion	Giraffe	Alligator
Star fish	Dolphin	Walrus
Tortoise	Frog	Duck
Penguin	Salamander	Shark

Land

Water

Try this!

Think of 3 questions you can ask your friend from the Venn diagram.

My Favourite Game

Ask your classmates if they like indoor games or outdoor games. Make a Venn diagram to record your observations.

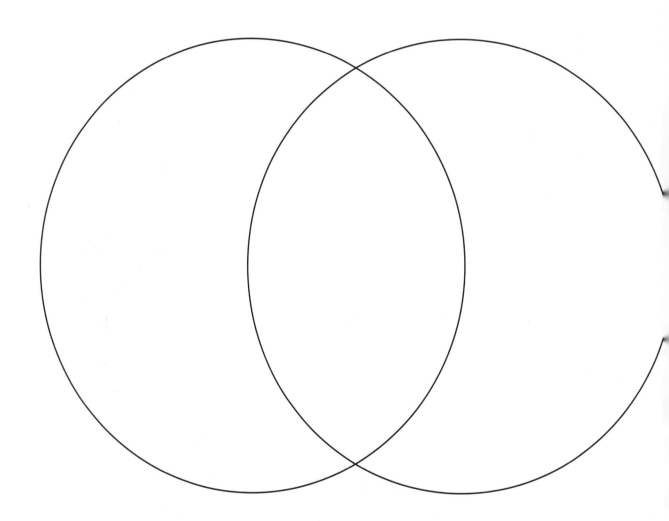

SCIENCE

Seeds

A seed is a baby plant that has a bundle of food all wrapped in a pack.

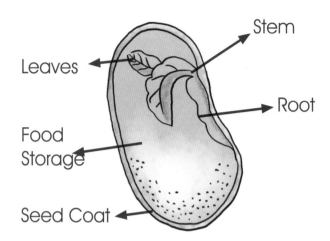

Leaves
Stem
Root
Food Storage
Seed Coat

What does a seed look like? Seeds have many different shapes and sizes.

Marigold seeds are small and thin. ▼

Marigold seeds

Marigold

Star Anise

▲

A pod is a shell for seeds. This pod has room for many seeds.

The peanut shell is hard and light brown.

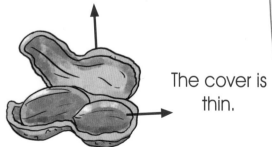

The cover is thin.

OBSERVE & INFER

Collect different seeds like wild rice, watermelon, lettuce, corn and other common ones and observe them. Make a chart to describe each one of them as shown here.

corn seed

It is yellow. It is about 1cm long. It is smooth. It is shaped like a raindrop.

We eat corn. Some animals eat corn seeds.

Growing Seeds

Seeds need water and air to sprout. When the seedling grows, it needs soil, water and sunlight to grow big and strong.

Draw a yellow sun. Draw blue water coming from a hose or watering can. Label the soil. Write the word air.

sprout   seedling   plant

Which Way Do I Grow?

Supplies:
glass jar with a screw lid
6 paper towels
water
2 green bean seeds
soaked in water overnight.

Directions:

Step1: Roll up six paper towels and place them in the glass jar.

Step2: Moisten the paper towels with water.

Step3: Insert two bean seeds between the paper towels and the glass so that each seed is visible from the outside of the jar as shown.

Step4: Place the jar in a warm, sunny area. In about three days. Observe that roots begin to grow down from the seeds as shown. Keep the paper towels moist.

Step5: When the roots are about one inch long and a shoot begins to push out, screw the lid on tight and turn the jar upside down. Record your observations.

Number the pictures from 1 to 5 to show growth of watermelon.

Soon a vine will be found.

Then a melon begins to show.

A seed is planted in the ground.

A yellow flower starts to grow.

Big and round as it can be.

a watermelon grew for you and me!

Seeds Scatter

For seeds to grow, they need to travel to new places in the ground. Here are some ways that they travel:

Some plants explode and send their seeds flying into the air.

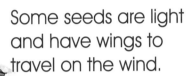

Some seeds are light and have wings to travel on the wind.

Some birds and animals can move seeds around and forget them in the ground.

Heavy seeds fall to the ground.

Some seeds have little hooks on them so they stick to an animal's fur and travel to a new place.

Many seeds are eaten by animals and are planted in their droppings.

Some seeds are hollow inside so that they can float on the water until they find a new place to grow.

Your turn

Find out how do these seeds travel?

blackberry, coconut, violet, wheat, dandelion, maple and sandbur

Seed Puzzle

Read each clue. Write the missing word in the puzzle. Use the word bank.

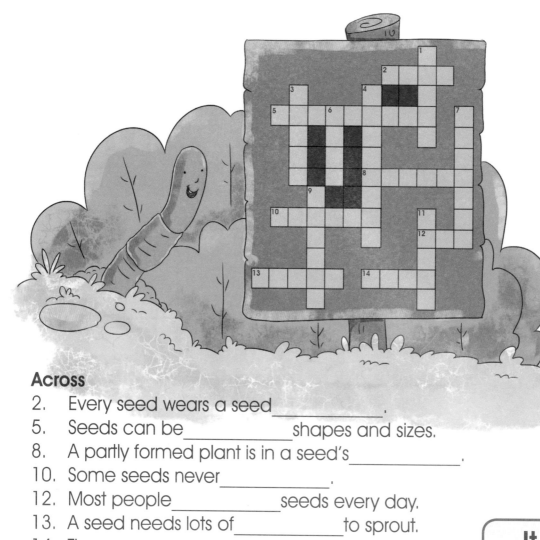

Word Bank

wind

different

coconut

eat

food

parts

embryo

coat

protects

seeds

water

light

travel

sprout

Across

2. Every seed wears a seed_____.
5. Seeds can be_____shapes and sizes.
8. A partly formed plant is in a seed's_____.
10. Some seeds never_____.
12. Most people_____seeds every day.
13. A seed needs lots of_____to sprout.
14. The_____scatters some seeds.

Down

1. Every seed has three_____.
3. Most seeds do not need_____to sprout.
4. The seed coat_____a seed.
6. Seeds have their own_____.
7. A_____is a big seed.
9. Seeds_____in many different ways.
11. Plants make_____.

It is True

Most seeds remain dormant (asleep) until they are given water.

Plant Parts and Functions

Plants usually have branches, leaves, stems and roots. They bear flowers, fruits and seeds. Most plants have leaves that are green.

Tick the statements that are true for each part of the plant.

Roots:

1. Fix the plant in the soil.
2. Carry water and minerals to other parts of the plant.
3. Some roots like carrot, turnip, radish and beetroot store food in them.

Stem:

1. Gives support to the plants.
2. Carries water and nutrients from the roots to the leaves.
3. Leaves, flowers, buds and fruits grow on the stem.

Leaves:

1. Make manure for the plant.
2. Help the plant breathe.
3. Store food.

Flowers:

1. Make seeds.
2. Attract insects and birds.
3. Store food.

Label the parts of the plant.

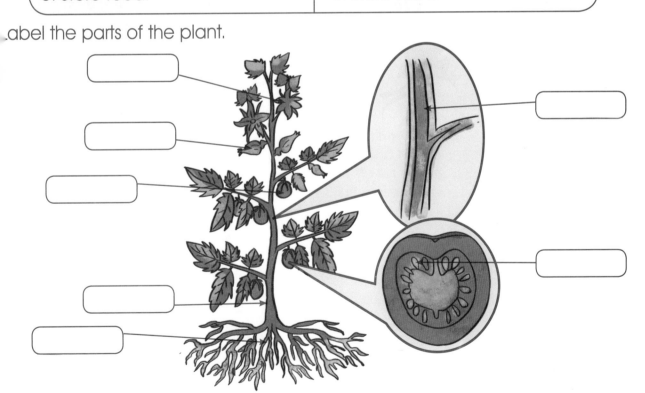

Flowers and Fruits

Inside a flower is a sticky powder called **pollen**. Pollen helps flowers make seeds.

Pollination

One part of the flower called the ANTHER makes pollen.

Another part of the flower, called the PISTIL leads to the eggs.

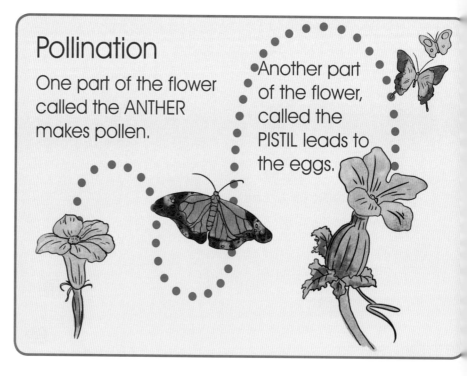

from here

to here

1. Pollen moves from one part of the flower to another.

2. The flower grows bigger and the petals fall off. It grows into a fruit.

3. The fruit protects the seeds inside.

4. When the fruit is ripe, it is ready to eat.

5. The seeds inside the fruit can grow into new plants.

Your turn

Find a plant to observe. Does the plant have flowers? Which sense did you use to find out?

Types of Plants

here are many different types of plants. Plants can be grouped according to the features they have in common.

Answer the riddles to find the names of different kinds of plants. Then choose the best example and look for the words in the word search.

1. I have thin woody stems and don't grow as tall as trees. _____ cotton/wheat

2. I have soft and green stems. I live only for a few months. _____ palm/mint

3. I am tall and strong with many branches. My fruits are hard on the outside but have water in it. _____ sunflower/coconut

4. I don't have strong stems so I crawl along the ground. _____ watermelon/grapevine

5. I need the support of another plant or sticks to stand. _____ maple/pea

```
W  W  M  I  N  T  L  V  Y  Y  Z  O  S  J  F
O  A  U  O  N  A  U  D  I  G  D  O  R  V  A
J  F  T  O  Q  W  A  T  E  R  M  E  L  O  N
L  V  Z  K  H  D  P  E  A  W  J  O  C  O  V
V  A  M  A  G  V  X  P  S  E  X  G  O  Q  I
I  G  R  F  I  F  T  W  H  N  N  J  T  V  B
X  W  H  W  C  O  C  O  N  U  T  T  J  H  G
T  L  U  C  L  E  S  H  D  U  Z  Q  N  M  X
Q  N  H  Y  B  L  P  H  L  E  K  E  S  V  T
X  Z  P  C  D  V  J  W  E  Y  H  Z  Q  Q  M
W  N  V  D  B  H  F  W  H  K  E  N  H  W  Y
O  G  F  K  Q  T  H  C  J  Z  V  Y  U  G  R
J  I  Z  B  I  F  H  I  L  N  L  Q  D  J  M
Y  C  D  L  S  C  P  L  X  I  C  Z  R  T  K
O  K  J  D  C  O  T  T  O  N  A  P  J  F  D
```

GRADE 2: SCIENCE

Adaptations in Plants

ants have different ways to stay safe and get what they need.

or example:

he willow tree has long roots to get water from deep in the ground. A actus has thorns to protect itself.

ok at each picture and write the special feature that each plant has.

_____ _____ _____ _____

It Is True

It's not only animals that eat plants but some plants are hungry for animals too! The Venus Flytrap has leaves that shut when an insect lands on it. The leaves open up when the insect is eaten up.

OBSERVE & INFER

Look for five plants and study the kind of special features they have. Make a table to record your observations. Then look for any bugs, brown or yellow spots on the leaves, curled leaves and stems or bark that looks like it has been chewed. Do these plants have any defence mechanism to protect themselves? How you do know?

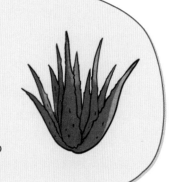

Insects

Insects are tiny animals that are commonly seen in our surroundings.

Insect body has 3 main parts – head, thorax and abdomen

head ←

thorax ←

abdomen ←

Insects have 6 legs and 2 antennae.

Some insects live together in colonies.

All insects lay eggs.

Some insects may sting or bite you.

Insects use antennae to hear, touch and smell with.

Brain tilt

Which of these are not insects? Why?

butterfly	centipede	ant
earthworm	wasp	spider
dragonfly	termite	dog tick
lady bug	tapeworm	fly

It Is True

Insects don't have bones. They have a hard covering called exoskeleton on the outside.

OBSERVE & INFER

Use the hand lens or microscope to look at a lady bug. What does it look like? What parts does it have? What do you think will happen if you touch the lady bug with the tip of a cotton swab? Gently touch the lady bug with the tip of a cotton swab. Describe what happened to the bug when you touched it with the cotton swab. Was your prediction correct?

How Do Insects Grow?

Complete the life cycle of the butterfly and fill in the blanks.

Insects start their life cycle as eggs. Their babies look totally different from them. The babies undergo amazing changes and grow to look just like their parents.

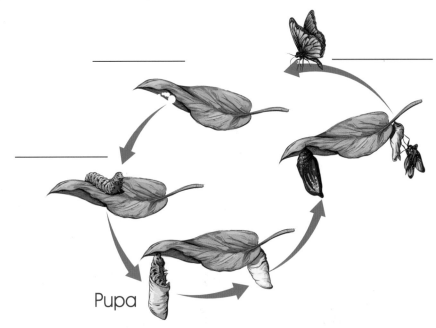

Pupa

1. The butterfly lays eggs on a _____.

2. The eggs hatch and _____ comes out.

3. The larva is also called a _____.

4. The larva sheds its _____ and begins to transform into a pupa.

5. After about _____ weeks, the pupa splits open and _____ comes out.

How do insects protect themselves?

Some insects _____ and _____ to protect themselves.

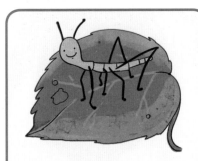

Some insects have _____ and _____ that blend with the hiding places.

Some insects taste _____ and so are not eaten by birds or other animals.

Spiders

Spiders are 8-legged animals with a two part body. They are not insects but arachnids.

Spider body has two parts – thorax and abdomen.

Spiders have fangs that are poisonous.

They don't have a separate head and antennae.

They feel things through the hair on their body.

Most spiders have eight eyes but some also have two, four or six eyes.

They spin web with their spinnerets.

They have an extra pair of short appendages.

Legs are connected to the front part of the body.

Complete the life cycle of a spider with the help of word bank.

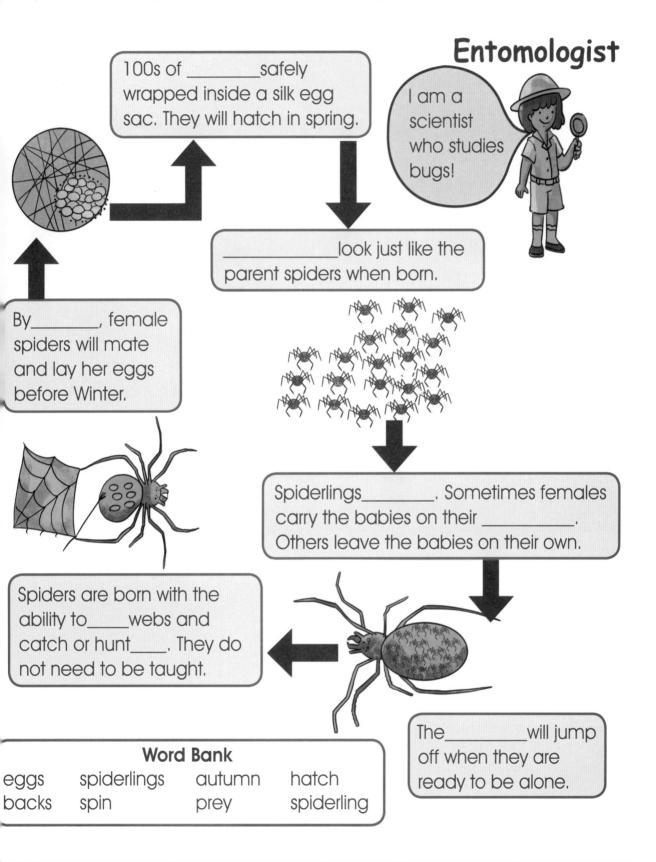

Entomologist

I am a scientist who studies bugs!

100s of _____ safely wrapped inside a silk egg sac. They will hatch in spring.

_____ look just like the parent spiders when born.

By_____, female spiders will mate and lay her eggs before Winter.

Spiderlings_____. Sometimes females carry the babies on their _____. Others leave the babies on their own.

Spiders are born with the ability to_____webs and catch or hunt____. They do not need to be taught.

The_____will jump off when they are ready to be alone.

Word Bank

eggs	spiderlings	autumn	hatch
backs	spin	prey	spiderling

Reptiles

Find names of seven reptiles in the word search.

```
F  A  K  I  J  G  E  F  N  P  S  J  U  P  K
S  I  T  I  S  S  R  M  I  F  P  T  D  D  Q
N  Z  M  J  P  K  P  E  Q  E  M  O  P  D  S
A  T  J  Z  T  I  G  U  A  N  A  R  D  I  C
K  L  X  S  J  N  Q  Z  B  H  O  T  Q  N  R
E  M  I  A  O  K  D  O  O  D  S  O  U  O  O
V  W  E  X  I  Q  J  V  W  Z  X  I  H  S  C
B  T  R  E  C  A  Q  I  U  Y  B  S  L  A  O
N  Y  A  J  N  Z  D  J  G  O  F  E  T  U  D
K  W  N  W  I  I  V  Z  S  X  F  Z  B  R  I
X  Z  A  M  C  L  G  Y  W  C  K  M  S  H  L
V  L  Q  Z  Z  C  H  A  M  E  L  E  O  N  E
K  Q  L  R  J  U  G  D  W  J  K  Q  G  M  A
R  X  N  O  D  A  L  L  I  G  A  T  O  R  V
V  P  Z  L  I  Z  A  R  D  V  D  K  Q  S  B
```

Write True or False.

1. Reptiles are warm-blooded animals. _____

2. Reptiles have scales on their body. _____

3. Most reptiles shed their skin. _____

4. Reptiles are vertebrates so they do not have bones. _____

5. Most reptiles lay eggs. _____

OBSERVE & INFER

Study about different reptiles and find:
How they are adapted to live in their habitat
What they do when it's extremely cold.
How they keep themselves safe.
Do they blend into their environment?
Form a report.

It Is True

Reptiles are cold-blooded animals which means their body temperature changes according to their surroundings. When it is warm outside they are warm and become cold when it is cold.

Complete the information about the reptiles below.

Snakes:

- Have _____ legs.
- Have a _____ sense of smell.
- _____ their skin.
- Shoot _____ or venom from their _____ into their prey to kill it.

Lizards:

- Move by _____.
- Eat _____, _____ and _____.
- Defend themselves by _____ when they are attacked.

Tortoises:

- Are the only reptiles with _____.
- Lay their eggs on _____.
- Eat _____.
- Pull their _____ and _____ into their shell when attacked.

Alligator vs Crocodile

Can you find the difference between a crocodile and an alligator? Well look at their snout and teeth. An alligator's snout is wider than a crocodile's. A crocodile has a pair of bottom teeth that show off even when its mouth is closed.

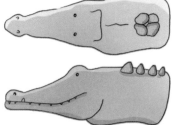

Your Turn

Why doesn't a lizard fall off even while it is walking on the ceiling? Find.

Amphibians

Amphibians are animals that:

- are cold-blooded
- have backbones and webbed feet
- breathe through lungs as adults and gills as young ones
- have moist smooth skin (no hair, fur or scales)
- live part of their lives in water and on land
- lay many eggs

Complete the life cycle of a frog.

Word Bank

jelly

froglet

gills

legs

frog

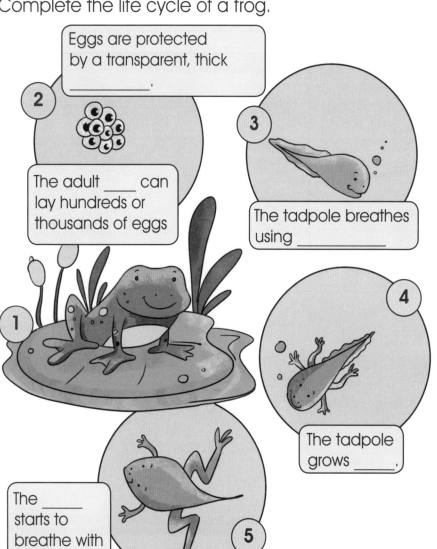

2 Eggs are protected by a transparent, thick _____.

The adult ____ can lay hundreds or thousands of eggs

3 The tadpole breathes using _____

4 The tadpole grows ____.

1

The ____ starts to breathe with lungs.

5

OBSERVE & INFER

Study about different characteristics of amphibians and reptiles. Make a comparison chart to show how they are alike and how they are different?

Birds

Birds have many unique features which are different from other animals.

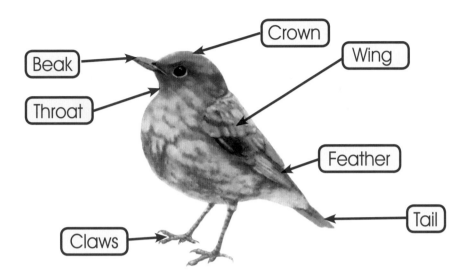

Fill in the blanks to complete the information about birds.

Birds:

1. have _____ on their bodies.

2. fly with the help of their _____.

3. have _____ muscles that help them to move their wings.

4. have a _____ shaped body that helps them to cut through the air.

5. have a _____ but no teeth.

6. have a light body because of _____ bones. This helps them to _____ easily.

Birds have different kinds of feet that help them to swim, wade and perch. Look at the feet of different birds. Give examples of birds with such feet. Some have been done for you.

Bird Beaks

Look at the picture and write the kind of beak each bird has. Take help of the word bank.

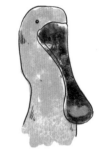

1._____

2._____

3._____

4._____

5._____

6._____

7._____

8._____

9._____

10._____

Word Bank			
small conical beak	long slender beak	hooked beak	slender
curved beak	slender beak	spatulate beak	sharp
beak	short curved and downward-facing beak		

Mammals

Mammals are animals that give birth to live young. They have hair or fur on their body. Mammal mothers nurse their young ones with milk. Mammals are warm-blooded, that means, they can maintain their body temperature.

Solve the riddles to find names of mammals in the word search.

I'm very, very big. I like to eat peanuts and hay.

I live in the ocean. I sing to my family and can breathe through a hole on the top of my head.

I have four legs. I like to smell things. I wag my tail when I am happy.

I'm very big and furry. I like to go on a sleep when winter is on a hurry.

I like to use my long tongue to eat leaves from tops of trees. I don't have to climb up though. With my long neck it's a breeze.

S	G	P	T	Z	A	K	J	W	W
E	Y	W	N	J	F	M	D	Q	N
J	K	K	K	V	Y	G	T	K	
A	Y	S	G	G	V	P	O	A	S
C	B	P	U	X	U	I	N	B	X
Q	K	Q	Q	N	H	D	O	G	W
E	I	D	B	D	B	E	A	R	L
E	L	E	P	H	A	N	T	M	W
D	O	L	P	H	I	N	F	G	P
H	G	I	R	A	F	F	E	N	Q

What Do Mammals Eat?

A mammal can be a carnivore, herbivore or omnivore.

Carnivore: an animal that eats flesh of other animals.

Herbivore: an animal that eats plants.

Omnivore: an animal that eats both plants and animals.

Fish

Fish are a group of
aquatic animals.

Fish don't
have lungs.

They are cold-
blooded animals.

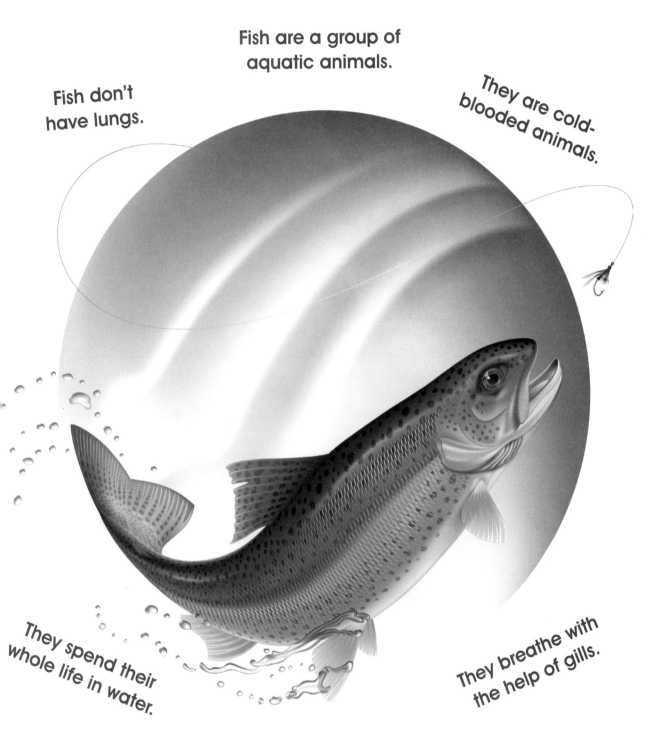

They spend their
whole life in water.

They breathe with
the help of gills.

The body of fish is covered with scales and shiny
coating. Fish reproduce by laying eggs.

Parts of a Fish

Fill in the blanks with the words from the word bank.

1. Most fish have _____ that cover their skin.

2. Scales help _____ fish.

3. Fish have special organs called _____ located on the sides of their head.

4. Gills are made of thin sheets or _____ and help the fish _____.

5. The fins of a fish help it to swim, _____, stop and _____.

6. The _____ fin is used for swimming.

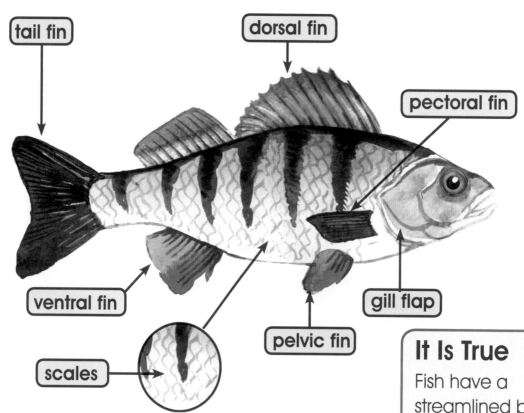

tail fin

dorsal fin

pectoral fin

ventral fin

gill flap

scales

pelvic fin

It Is True

Fish have a streamlined body i.e. pointed snout and rear. This helps the fish swim efficiently through the water.

Word Bank

steer	balance	gills	membranes
scales	protect	breathe	tail

Weather

Weather is the state of the atmosphere that tells if it is hot or cold, wet or dry, calm or stormy, clear or cloudy.

What makes weather?

There are many factors that make weather happen. Look at the picture below and write the names of the factors in the correct place.

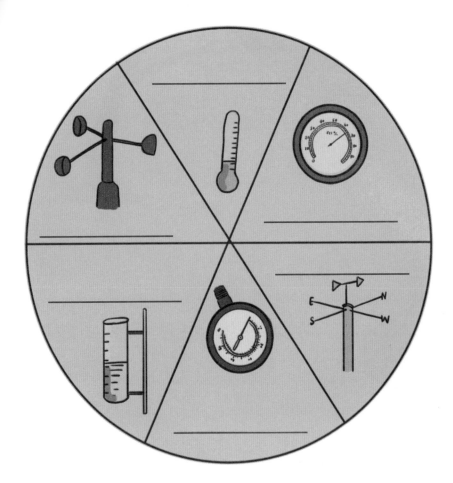

Word Bank

Pressure

Humidity

Temperature

Wind speed

Precipitation

Wind direction

Identify the instruments and write their names below.

_____   _____   _____

Fill in the blanks to complete the information about factors that make weather happen.

 Temperature is how _____ or cold it is. We use a _____ to measure temperature. The _____ the weather, the higher the liquid in a thermometer rises.

Wind is _____ air. The Sun's heat ____ up the air and it _____ up. _____ air takes its place. This happens over and over again and we feel the air as _____ .

Humidity is the amount of _____ in the air. Water in the _____, seas, lakes and rivers is _____ by the Sun. Some of it evaporates and turns into a gas called _____

Wind and Weather

The _____ of air pushing on the earth is called air pressure.

Word Bank			
cold	thermometer	moisture	weight
warmer	oceans	moving	hot
warms	wind	rises	heated

Magic Water Glass

You will need

A glass

Water

Index card

What to do?

- Fill a glass one-third with water.

- Cover the mouth with an index card and invert (holding the card in place) over a sink.

- Remove your hand from the card.

What happened?

The card stays in place because air is heavier than water. The card stays in place because of air pressure. The air under the card pushes it strongly and keeps the card in place. The water pushes the card down but the air pressure is higher than the pressure of water!

Water Cycle

The water on the earth keeps going around and around in a continuous cycle in what we call the "Water Cycle". In this cycle the water circulates between the Earth's oceans, atmosphere, and land, and returns to the atmosphere by evaporation and transpiration.

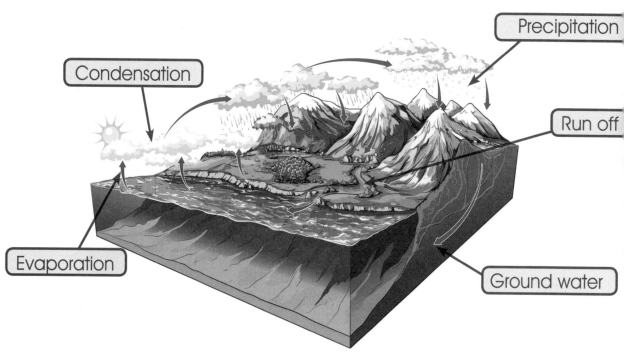

Match the label to the definition.

Evaporation	A change of phase from liquid to solid.
Transpiration	The process by which surface water enters the soil.
Condensation	A change of state from a liquid to a gas.
Precipitation	The loss of water from plants and vegetation.
Infiltration	The name given to condensed water vapour falling from the sky. Most occurs as rain, snow and hail.

Force

Force is a push or pull.

Pull

Push

What can force do?

Force can change
the state of motion
of a moving body.

Force can move a body at rest.

It can sometimes change
the size or shape of a body.

OBSERVE & INFER

Kick a football hard.
What type of force do you use?
Can you describe other sports or
activities that involve push and pull?

Force

Paste pictures of some things you can:

Push

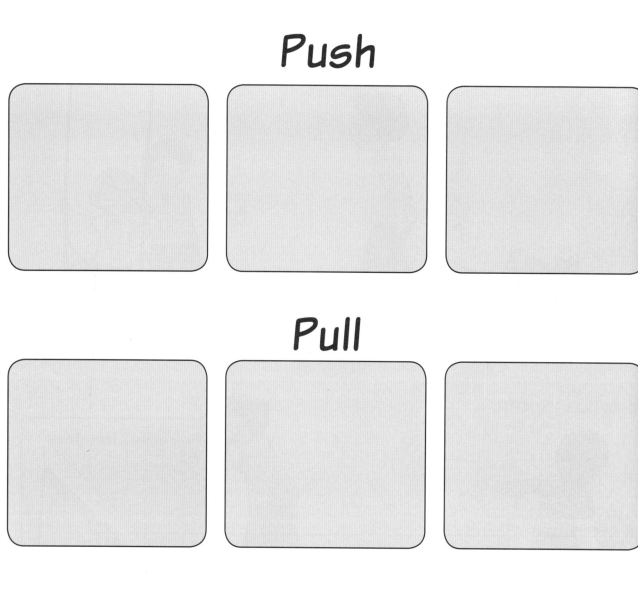

Pull

Both Push and Pull

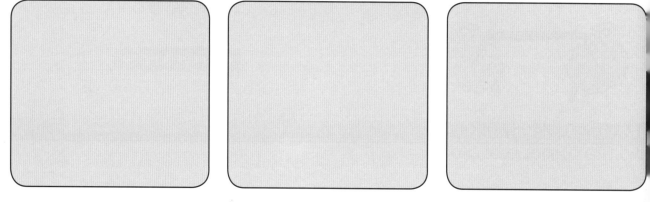

SOCIAL SCIENCES

Family

A family is a unit of parents and their children living together.

Look at the pictures and write what families do together.

Draw your family doing something together.

Family

This is Jack's family. Use these words to label the picture.

> father, mother, grandfather, grandmother, brother, sister

James

Doris

Linda

Neo

Alice

Jack

Write if these statements are true or false.

1. James is Jack's grandfather. ———————

2. Linda is Alice's daughter. ———————

3. Neo is James's father. ———————

4. Jack is Doris's grandson. ———————

5. Alice is James's wife. ———————

6. Doris is Linda's grandmother. ———————

7. James is Linda's father. ———————

8. Jack is Alice's son. ———————

Our Needs and Wants

Needs are things without which it would be difficult to live or survive.

Wants are things we would like to have but don't need to live.

Draw a line from the word to the picture it goes with.

1. need
2. want

3. need
4. want

5. need
6. want

7. need
8. want

We Live in a Neighbourhood ▬

Look at the drawing of Nancy's neighbourhood and fill in the blanks.

A neighbourhood is a place where people live. Every neighbourhood has homes, school, shops and other places.

Sterling Apartments

Park

Bus stop

Grocery store

Cleaner's shop

Hardware shop

Dau Cleaners

1. Nancy's neighbourhood has a _____, _____, park, _____ and _____.
2. Nancy lives in _____.
3. _____ is to the left of Nancy's apartments.
4. Nancy and her friends play in the _____.
5. Her neighbourhood belongs to a _____.

Community

A community is a place where people live and work together for the common good. There are three types of communities – urban, suburban and rural.

Urban

- Many people live close together
- Small amount of space
- Less open areas or natural areas
- Tall skyscrapers

- Close to, but not, in cities
- Fewer people
- Small apartments but no Skyscrapers

Suburban

Rural

- Fewer people
- A few buildings spread over large distances
- Lots of open space and natural areas

Try this! Make a comparison chart to show things that are similar and different in urban, suburban and rural areas.

My Community

Answer these questions about your community.

1. What is the name of your community?_____

2. Where is it located?_____

3. Which large city is it near?_____

4. Are there any historical monuments? If so, name them and state where are they located.

    a. _____

    b. _____

5. What is unique about your community?

    a. _____

    b. _____

6. Why do you like your community?

    a. _____

    b. _____

Draw a picture of the community you live in. Write a sentence to describe it.

Goods and Services in a Community

Goods are things that people make or grow.
For example: crops, soap, jute bags
Services are jobs or work that other people do for you.
For example: a barber cuts hair, so he provides us a service.

Goods
apples for sale

Service
a barber cutting hair

Write goods or services for the pictures given below..

_____   _____   _____

_____   _____   _____

Help!

There are many community services that help you in different ways. Which one should you call for each problem below?

Draw a line to match the need with the place that meets it.

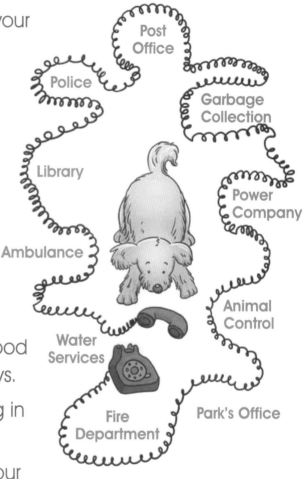

1. You need help finding a fact for your science homework.

2. You see a fire out of your window.

3. You find a lost bag on the street.

4. You want to use the park for your cricket team party.

5. Someone has been hurt.

6. You need to find a zip code.

7. You see a leaking water pipe in your locality.

8. The garbage in your neighbourhood has not been picked up for 3 days.

9. There is a dangerous dog straying in your neighbourhood.

10. The electricity has gone out on your street.

Post Office

Police

Garbage Collection

Library

Power Company

Ambulance

Animal Control

Water Services

Fire Department

Park's Office

Try this!

It is Saturday and Norman has a lot to do today. He has to go to the library to find a book about transport. Then he has to go to the clinic to get medicine for Granny. Next, he has to buy some postage stamps for his Mom. Lastly, for his Dad, he has to find out what time the soccer game starts. Name all services Norman would use.

Rules in a Community

Just as we have rules in the family, we need to follow certain rules and laws in our community to keep ourselves safe and peaceful.

Write agree or disagree for these rules in the community.

1. No talking in the library.

2. No driving while operating a mobile phone.

3. All owners of television sets must have a licence.

4. No littering in shopping malls.

5. Spitting chewing gum in public places.

6. Walk on the track in a park.

7. Ignore traffic signals if you are in a hurry.

8. No seat belts while driving.

9. Playing loud music in the neighbourhood.

10. Park your car anywhere in the market.

 Think about it

You are walking around the supermarket and are very hungry so you pick up a bar of chocolate; you eat it and throw away the wrapper before you exit. Is this OK?

Rules in a Community

Look at the picture and talk to your friend about it.

. Who has broken a rule in this picture?

_____

. What has the driver of the yellow car done that is wrong?

_____

. What do you think the traffic police officer should do?

_____

What should you do when you see someone breaking a rule in the school?

Community Signs and Symbols

We see different signs and symbols around us. These signs and symbols keep us safe and also aware of the community.

NO BIKES

Look at these signs and symbols. Write the name of each sign. Choose from the help box.

_____ _____ _____ _____ _____

_____ _____ _____ _____ _____

_____ _____ _____ _____ _____

Help Box

Railroad Crossing	Stop	Bike Route	Caution
Handicapped	No Pedestrian	Phone	No Bike
School Crossing	Men	Women	Exit
Bus Stop	Hospital	Emergency	Walk

People Communicate

Communication means sending information from one person to another. Talking is the most common way of communicating that we all know.

We can also communicate by other ways such as:

writing letters

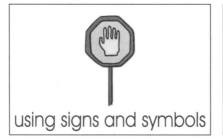
using signs and symbols

email

newspapers

books

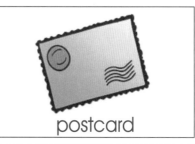
postcard

telephone

radio

television

fax

music

advertisements

Think about it

Look at these words and sentences. We can tell someone all these things without talking. Take turns with your friend to show how we communicate each one.
1. Come here 2. No 3. Quiet 4. I am angry 5. Stop

People Communicate

Look at the picture. How many different ways of communication can you find?

1. How many people are reading something?

   _____

2. What kind of reading can we do for fun?

   _____

3. What do we read every day to find what is happening in our city and country?

   _____

4. What kind of communication is the "wet paint"?

   _____

5. Name one warning sign you see in the picture.

   _____

People Communicate

ck the correct option in each sentence.

. We get stamps from the **(newspaper office/post office).**
. **(Letters/ e-mails)** are sent through internet.
. **(Telephone/Television)** is the fastest means of communication.
. We can carry **(telephones/mobile phones)** with us.
. A **(letter/television)** is a means of mass communication.
. You can find lots of information on any subject in a **(postcard/book).**
. A **(e-mail/newspaper)** is a printed means of communication.

retend you are on holiday in a town that you have not been to before.
Vrite a postcard to your friend about everything you have seen
and done.

Using Transportation

We use different kinds of transport to get from one place to another and to move things from one place to another. There are many different kinds of transport. Most of us travel on land by roads, trains and footpaths. We also use roads and trains to transport things on land.

In each sentence below, cross the information that is wrong. Correct the sentences and rewrite them.

1. Thousands of years ago, man used to travel from one place to another using a car.

   _____

2. In rural areas, people usually travel by bullet trains.

   _____

3. Dogs were used to pull carts some years ago.

   _____

4. Things like coal, vehicles and goods are transported by passenger trains.

   _____

5. The fastest means of transportation is train.

   _____

6. A yacht is a ship that remains inside the water.

   _____

7. Trains run on steel tracks that are called cars.

   _____

8. A helicopter can carry large number of people.

   _____

Mapping My Neighbourhood

map is a drawing of a place. Maps can be drawn to represent a
ariety of information such as roads, directions, places and more.

map has:

Big Island

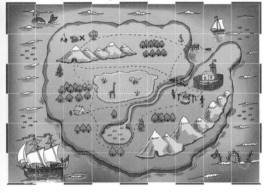

a title
name given to the map

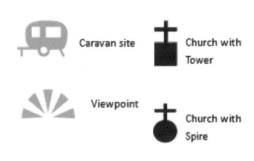

symbols
can be line, shape or colour

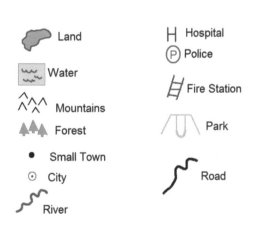

legend or key
tell what the symbols mean

compass rose
shows direction on a map

Pictures and Maps

The model below shows Kate's community from an aeroplane. Study it and answer the questions.

Kate's Community

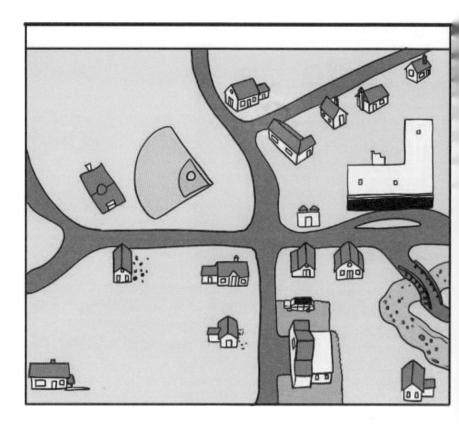

Circle the map that shows Kate's community..

Map A

Map B

Pictures and Maps

olly and her friends are playing hide and seek. Help her find her friends
by looking at the map. Answer the questions.

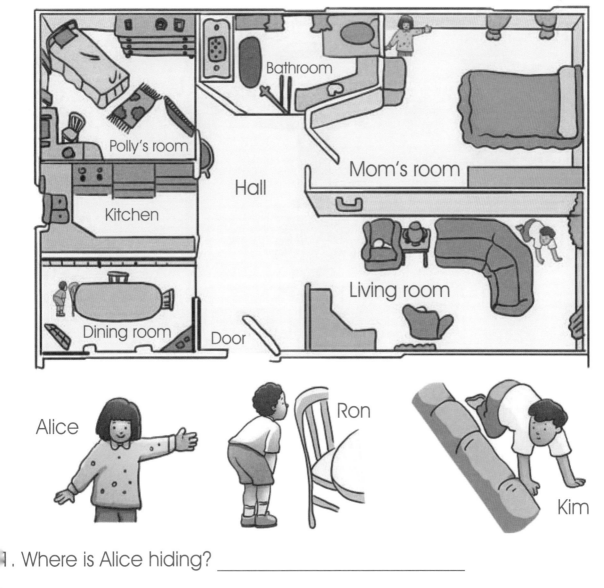

Bathroom

Polly's room

Hall

Mom's room

Kitchen

Living room

Dining room

Door

Alice

Ron

Kim

1. Where is Alice hiding? _____

2. Who is in the dining room? _____

3. Who is hiding in the room next to Mom's room? _____

4. Where is Polly's room? Circle it. _____

5. How many rooms does Polly's house have? _____

Finding Directions on a Map

Look at the picture and answer the questions.

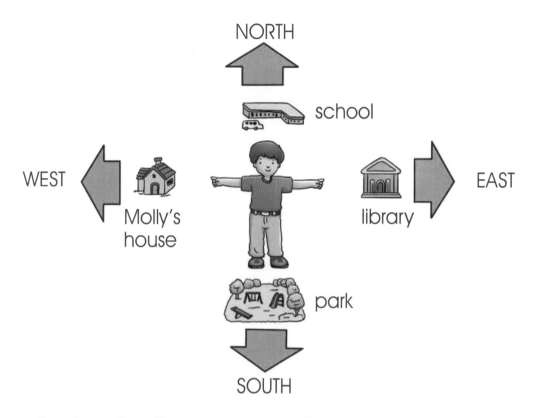

1. Name the four directions you see on the map.

   _____

2. In which direction should Daniel walk to go to school?

   _____

3. In which direction is the library?

   _____

4. Daniel wants to go to the park. In which direction should he move?

   _____

5. Molly's house is to the _____ of Daniel.

Try this! Stand in front of your house facing the north. Name the places that are to your east, west and south.

Map of the Zoo

Look at the map of the zoo. Then answer the questions.

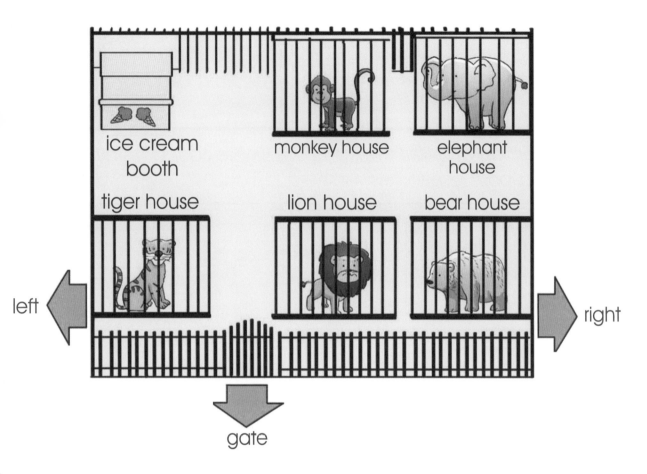

1. Which house is to the right of the ice cream booth?

_____

2. Which house is to the left of lion's house?

_____

3. Which house is to the right of monkey's house?

_____

4. How many houses are to the right of tiger's house?

_____

5. If you stand where the bear is, which house would be to your right and left?

_____

Using a Compass Rose

A compass rose is a figure on a compass, map, chart or monument used to show directions: North, East, South and West.

Compass rose

Look at the map and find the campsite where Jacob is staying. Then use the compass rose to answer the questions.

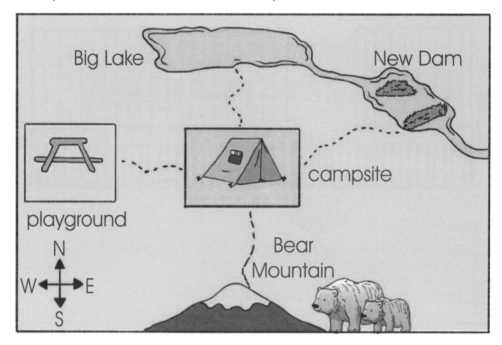

1. In which direction should Jacob walk to reach the playground?

_____

2. Is the Bear Mountain to the west or south of the campsite?

_____

3. In which direction should Jacob walk to reach the Big Lake?

_____

4. Is the New Dam east or west of the Big Lake?

_____

Using Map Symbols

ook at the map of a community below. Use the map and map
ymbols to answer the questions.

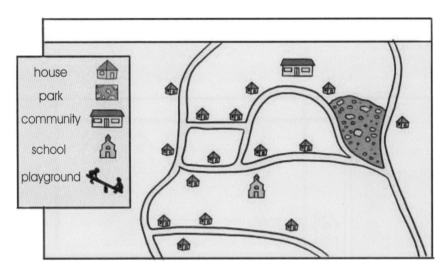

. There are many houses in the community. Which symbol stands for
   a house?

2. What is to the east of the park? Circle it on the map.

_____

3. What is the symbol of the community centre? Draw it here.

_____

4. How many schools do you see on the map? Put a (✓) on the map.

_____

5. Which symbol shows the playground?

Try this! Draw a line to show the route you can take to reach the school from the community centre. Which directions you moved in?

Using a Map Key

A map key helps to study the information needed for the map to make sense. It explains what symbols or colours on a map mean.

Look at the map key. Find the symbols and circle them. Then answer the questions.

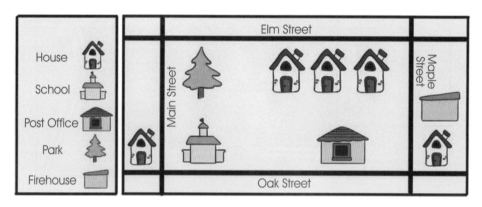

1. Which symbol stands for the park?

2. Which symbol stands for the firehouse?

3. How many houses can you see on the map?

_____

4. Name the streets on the map.

_____

5. Find the post office on the map and circle it.

Try this! Make a map showing any 5 places around your neighbourhood. Use your own symbols and key.

Studying a Map

Look at the map carefully. Then answer the questions.

1. Which seas are to the west of England?

_____

2. In which direction is Scotland from England?

_____

3. In which direction should you move from Ireland to go to England?

_____

4. Draw the symbols that show the mountains and river.

_____

5. How many rivers do you see on the map? Name them.

_____

Landforms and Water

A landform is a natural feature of the Earth's surface.

River

Mountain

Hill

Pond

Desert

Coast

Lake

Plain

Valley

Ocean

Try this! How are a mountain, a hill and a valley different from one another?

GRADE 2: SOCIAL SCIENCE

Landforms and Water

Look at the drawing of different landforms and write the word used to describe:

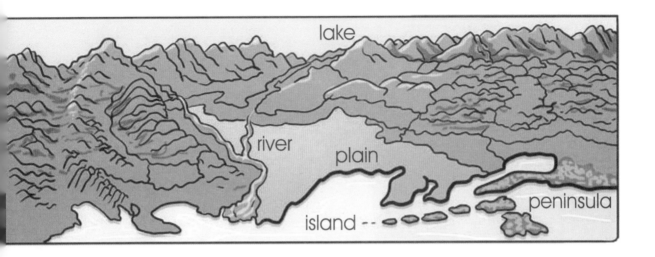

1. An area of land with water all around it.

_____

2. A water body with land all around it.

_____

3. A flat land.

_____

4. A large natural stream of water flowing in a channel to the sea.

_____

5. An area of land surrounded by water on three sides.

_____

Try this! Use your own words to define: a desert, a pond, a coast

Natural Resources

Natural resources are materials or substances occurring in nature which can be used by us.

For example: land, water, soil, sunlight

Look at the pictures. Put a tick on the natural resources.

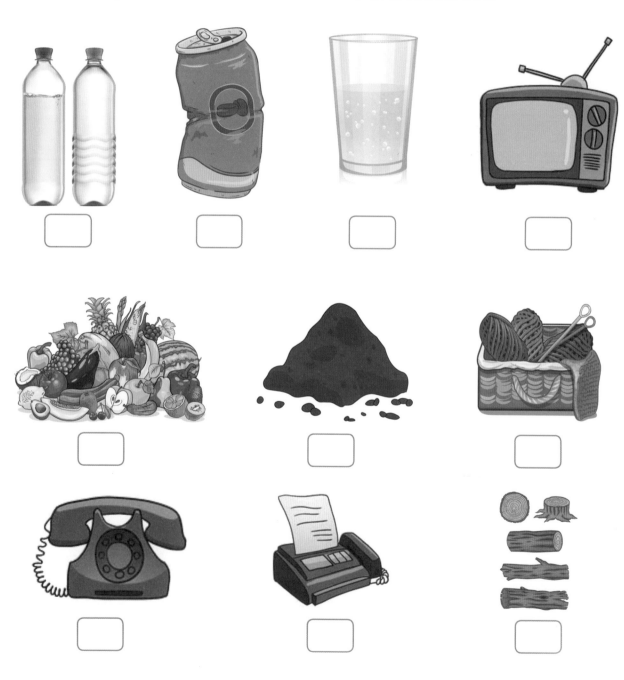

Taking Care of Natural Resources

Pick the picture that shows ways to care for natural resources.

Throw litter on the ground

Throw litter in the trash can

Use things again

Take care of birds and animals

Help to keep the surroundings clean

Answer Key

Page 2
1. hop, mop, pop, top
2. bench, flower, grass, tree
3. cap, jacket, shoes, trousers
4. bread, cupcake, pastry

Page 3

B	I	R	T	H	D	A	Y
J	O	L	G	I	F	T	S
F	R	O	S	T	I	N	G
K	T	L	H	A	P	P	Y
L	H	L	O	C	A	K	E
M	W	I	S	H	R	O	A
N	J	P	E	I	T	K	A
O	M	O	F	D	Y	R	V
P	I	P	C	F	E	W	D
I	C	E	C	R	E	A	M

Alphabetical order of the words:
birthday, cake, frosting , gifts,
happy, ice cream, lollipop,
party, wish

Page 4
Food - pasta, eggs, cornflakes,
patty, cheese, toast, noodles,
butter, almonds, kiwi, bread,
Drinks - milk, tea, coffee, water

Page 5

Women in the family	Places	Things you wear	Parts of your face	Size words
grandmother aunt daughter mother	market bank zoo airport	shoes jacket gloves trousers	eyebrows nose lips cheeks	short tall big long

Page 6

book	rain	light	bird	goat	squirrel
cars	magazine	sun	grass	ladybug	orange
clock	chair	newspaper	pillow	quilt	blanket
vest	sick	squid	drill	grandma	cucumber
huge	happy	octopus	square	eggplant	sea
giant	healthy	drawers	spinach	wise	sleep
woods	cookies	twelve	lake	pond	stream
sky	mountain	forest	indigo	pink	poppy
sausage	tomato	trousers	bark	branch	nest

Page 7
Odd one out in each group is:
1. secretary
2. uncle
3. smart
4. Thursday
5. tawny
6. ducklings

Page 8
1. glass, cup
2. watch, see
3. pay, buy
4. draw, paint
5. young, new
6. know, sure
7. cross, angry

Page 9
1. the floor
2. a pet
3. run
4. calf
5. a jump
6. yanking
7. a wind
8. at night

Page 10
1. cry
2. silent
3. warm
4. far
5. difficult
6. start
7. alone
8. true
9. quick
10. rich

hot
hard
fast
weep
correct
wealthy
quiet
begin
lonely
distant

Page 11
speak- talk
big- large
present- gift
shout- yell
loud- noisy
sweet- sugary

Page 12

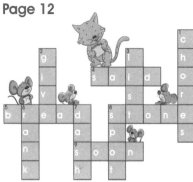

Page 13
1. quiet- noisy
2. tidiness- mess
3. loose-tight
4. shallow- deep
5. deny- accept
6. none-every
7. shrink- grow
8. polite- rude

Page 14
hide- seek
reach-leave
lose-win
repair- break
enter-exit
add- remove
strong- weak

Page 15
1. lost
2. difficult
3. never
4. dislikes
5. lost
6. sour
7. disagreed
8. common
9. foolish
10. new

Page 16
news, paper
lunch, box
air, plane
pan, cake
blue, berry
bath, robe
key, board
arm, chair
thunder, storm
water, melon

Children to make new words on their own.

Page 17

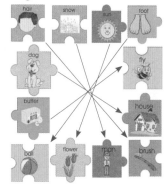

Page 18
1. toothpick
2. doghouse
3. cupcakes
4. cowboy
5. everything
6. backyard
7. breakfast
8. playground
9. pineapple
10. mailbox

Page 20
Children will do or their own.

Page 21
1. unwrap
2. preheat
3. return
4. unable
5. untied
6. redo
7. misspell
8. dishonest

Answer Key

First exercise

1. mostly
2. beautifully
3. tourist
4. coldest
5. movable
6. lately
7. driver

Second exercise

1. hopeful
2. unity
3. careless
4. weakness
5. useful
6. portable
7. beautiful
8. warmest
9. droopy
10. wisdom

Page 24

1. rewrite
2. misread
3. careless
4. agreeable
5. kindness
6. disappear
7. misuse
8. uncovered
9. sickness
10. dishonest
11. unfair
12. helpful

Page 26

right-write
piece-peace
night-knight
ate-eight
which-witch

Page 27

bee - bee
break - brake
– eye
knot- not
main - mane
ate - eight

dew - due
no- know
blew- blue
hair- hare
week- weak
some- sum
roll- role
pain- pane
right- write

Page 28

1. rode
2. paws
3. passed
4. board
5. won

Children will make sentences on their own.

Page 30

Children will do on their own.

Page 32

1. S
2. N
3. S
4. N
5. S
6. N
7. S
8. S

Page 33
Naming parts

1. Father and Carl
2. The day
3. The water
4. Carl
5. He
6. Carl
7. Father

Page 34
Telling part

1. help mom in the kitchen
2. makes rice and fish for supper
3. wipes the plates
4. lays the table for supper
5. are happy
6. like to work together

Page 35
Only sentence 2 is in correct order

1. Lia has a pet dog.
2. Her dog is a pug named Tuff.
3. Tuff is only one year old.
4. It has a soft brown coat.
5. It is fond of eating bread and milk.
6. Lia has made a kennel for Tuff.
7. Lia takes her dog for a walk in the evening.
8. Lia takes good care of Tuff.

Page 36

1. Many people like to fly kites.
2. Kites are made of paper.
3. A kite is shaped like a diamond.
4. Nick likes to fly kites too.
5. He has made a kite shaped like a bird.
6. It is fun to fly kites.

Page 37

1. Mary and her family went to the zoo.
2. How far is the zoo?
3. They reached there in two hours.
4. Which animals did Mary see in the zoo?
5. Did they see the white tiger?
6. They had fun at the zoo

Page 38

1. St
2. Q
3. St
4. St
5. Q
6. St
7. Q
8. St
9. Q
10. St

Page 39

1. Jim and Tim went to the Shoe House.
2. The Shoe House was so big!
3. The boys ran inside the house.
4. Oh, it was beautiful!
5. Jim and Tim were happy.
6. They played in the Shoe House.
7. It was awesome!

Page 40

1. Pick up apples, strawberries, cherries and pomegranate
2. Wash all the fruits.
3. Cut cherries into half and remove its pit.
4. Peel the pomegranate.
5. Chop apples and strawberries into small pieces.
6. Put sugar and cream in a bowl and mix it.
7. Now add all the fruits and mix well.

Page 41

1. Amy looked around the garden. St
2. Was someone hiding in the bushes? Q
3. Amy had a ball in his hands. St
4. Oh, he dropped the ball! E
5. He bent to pick up the ball. St
6. There were footprints on the mud. St
7. Who was there? Q
8. Don't move. C
9. Oh, it was a puppy! E
10. Amy lifted the puppy in his hands St

Page 42

Person	Place	Animal	Thing
Jim	house	lion	book
doctor	pool	dog	pen
Kate	school	fish	comb
Sim	mall	hen	chair

Page 43
Nouns

Pat, Neo, camp, boys, bag, shirts, shorts, socks, shoes, hat, books, toys, hills, sun, birds, bees, sheep, girls, boat

Page 44

1. tortoise
2. river
3. places
4. wings
5. stick, beaks
6. mouth
7. birds

Answer Key

Page 45

	b	u	s	h	e	s						
									f			
			w						o		b	
	p	e	a	c	h	e	s		x		r	
			t						e		u	
			c		d	r	e	s	s	e	s	
			h								h	
	b	u	s	e	s						e	
			s	a	n	d	w	i	c	h	e	s

Page 46
1. monkeys   2. toys   3. babies
4. cherries   5.stories   6. berries
7. days   8. trays   9. cities   10. ways

Page 47
1. calves   2. elves
3. halves   4. chefs
5. wolves   6. lives
7. giraffes   8. leaves
9. cliffs   10. selves
11. shelves   12. roofs
13. thieves   14. wives
15. schiefs

Page48
woman – women
mouse – mice
fish – fish
goose – geese
child – children
ox – oxen
sheep – sheep
deer – deer
dice – dice
tooth – teeth

Page 49
1. (an) apple and (a) pineapple
2. (a) monkey and (an) elephant
3. (a) banana and (an) orange
4. (an) ostrich and (an) owl

1. a   2. a, an 3. an   4. a
5. a   6. a, a, an, a, a   7. as

Page 50
Begin these words with capital

Jojo, Tim, Mary, Popo, Doyo, Joy, Kate, Neo, Linda

Page 51
Children will do on their own.

Page 52
Children have to attempt on their own. Answers will vary.

Page 53
1.   Toy Story
2.   The Chocolate Factory
3.   Pokemon
4.   The Little Mermaid

Children have to fill information about their mother. Answers will vary.

Page 54
Verbs:

1. helps   2.mows   3.pulls
4. picks   5.paint   6.gives

The birds chirp.
The wind blows.
The river flows.
Rabbits hop.
Girls sing.
And we stop!

Page 55
1. is   2. are   3. are   4. is
5. is, are 6. am   7. are   8. are

Page 56
1. was   2. were   3. were   4. was
5. were   6. were   7. was   8. were

Page 57
1. has   2. have   3. has   4. has
5. have   6. has   7. has   8. has

1.   Jenny had a party yesterday.
2.   She had a crown on her head.
3.   Her friends had flowers on their hair.

Page 58
1. He   2. It   3. He   4. It
5. He   6. It   7. He   8. They

Page 59
1. They are going to the sea shore.
2. Did they see the shark?

3. Sharks don't eat people, so we are not in danger.
4. Mom and Jags want to see snails. They are so cute!
5. "Have you ever seen a snail?" asked Mom.
6. They also saw a crab.
7. They always walk sideways.
8. "We are having so much fun on the shore," said Jags to mom.

Page 60
1. Mom and I went to see a magic show.
2. The usher gave me a ticket and showed us where to sit.
3. I could see the rabbits coming out of the hat.
4. We also saw paper flowers changing to roses.
5. We had great time!
6. I hope Mom takes me to another show soon!

Page 62
1. Him
2. He
3. Her
4. She
5. He, him
6. He

Page 63
1. they
2. they
3. them
4. they
5. they
6. they
7. their
8. they

Page 64
Possessive pronoun
My, your, their, his, her
Not a possessive pronoun
I, we, they, she, them, he

Page 65
1. my
2. his
3. his
4. our
5. his
6. my
7. her
8. her

Page 66
1. my
2. her
3. his
4. our
5. your
6. Your
7. its
8. its

Answer Key

The pronouns in bold are incorrect.

What is **yours** favourite thing to do in summer vacation?
Correct form - your.

Mine family visits a different theme park every summer.
Correct form- My.

Yang has **his'** own idea building a theme park. Correct form - his.

There would be only roller coasters in **his's**. Correct form - his.

Millie said that **her** would have water rides and a veggie park.
Correct form - her.

I would have a mix of everything in **mine's**. Correct form - mine.

That ride is fun because of **it's** fast speed. Correct form - its.

Next vacation my parents and I will visit **ours** favourite theme park.
Correct form - our.

Page 68
1. buy
2. look
3. tells
4. reads
5. like
6. chooses
7. want
8. tastes

Page 69
1. are
2. have
3. is
4. has
5. has
6. are
7. is
8. has
9. has
10. are

Page 70
1. grow
2. plants
3. watch
4. buzz
5. begins
6. help
7. choose
8. scoops
9. bakes
10. love

Page 71
Dad and I **go** to the library. He **reads** how to grow carrots. I read A Kid's Guide to Gardening. The **book** tells us how to grow a garden. We **want** to plant carrots, beans and potatoes. We **know** it takes hard work. For a while, it seems that nothing happens. We **wait** patiently, and soon green shoots appear. One day I **see** some white blossoms. I like gardening.

Page 72
1. We'll
2. We're
3. It's
4. He'll
5. Let's
6. Who'll
7. They've
8. You're

Page 73
1. don't
2. it's
3. aren't
4. there's
5. didn't
6. doesn't
7. haven't
8. isn't
9. who's
10. that's

Page 74
1. their
2. they're
3. it's
4. their
5. you're
6. your
7. its
8. it's

Page 75
I'm Rosa. I want to become a zoologist. **That's** someone who studies animals. Until then I will learn about animals by watching and reading. There are plenty of rabbits in our backyard. **They've** built their warren near the fence. **I've** seen rabbits hop across the yard. Then suddenly **they're** gone down the hole into the warren. I **can't** go down there! So I read about what **it's** like inside. Then I drew a picture of it.

Page 76
1st para
cute, brown, light, smooth, long, friendly
2nd para:
little, white, black, short, slender, striped

Page 77
1. small, sunken
2. west
3. prickly
4. shallow
5. dark
6. round
7. five, small, tallest
8. deep, hard

Page 78
1. three
2. ten
3. a few
4. nine
5. one
6. many

Page 79
smaller	taller
warmer	cooler
brighter	thicker
harder	longer
softer	thinner
smarter	slower
quieter	darker

Page 80
1. new
2. lower
3. warmer
4. softer
5. cheaper
6. smaller
7. high
8. wider
9. nicer
10. clean

Page 81
1. grandest
2. taller
3. louder
4. fanciest
5. plumper
6. smallest
7. bigger
8. happiest

Page 82
1. greatest
2. lighter
3. faster
4. quicker
5. youngest
6. fastest
7. taller
8. harder
9. greatest
10. biggest

Page 83
1. Verb- spoke, adverb- enthusiastically
2. Verb- listened, adverb- carefully
3. Verb- pulled, adverb- gently
4. Verb- moved, adverb- suddenly
5. Verb- cheered, adverb- loudly
6. Verb- bowed, adverb- gracefully

Page 84
1. verb: walks, adverb: toward
2. verb: holds, adverb: firmly
3. verb: hides, adverb: behind
4. verb: scared, adverb: yesterday
5. verb: remembers, adverb: today
6. verb: moves, adverb: quietly
7. verb: takes, adverb: now
8. verb: roars, adverb: loudly
9. verb: stand, adverb: still
10. verb: sneak, adverb: away

How?	When?	Where?
Firmly	Yesterday	Away
Quietly	Today	Toward
Loudly	Now	behind
Still		

Page 85
Children will do on their own.

Page 86
1. absolutely
2. mostly
3. carefully
4. very
5. quickly
6. greedily
7. lovingly
8. gently

Page 87
1. early
2. first
3. then
4. next
5. now
6. never
7. late
8. last

Answer Key

Page 88
Children will do on their own.

Page 89
Children will do on their own,

Page 94-107
Children will do on their own

Page 93
1. A Sunny Day
2. Too Much Traffic
3. Running a Race

Page 108

next   last   first

last   first   next

Page 112
Mac, Polly

Children will write the beginning, middle and end on their own.

Words used to describe tent, snacks and noises are:

Tent: big

Snacks: tasty

Noises: scary

Page 113:
1. Ollie, the owl
2. Paula at the Pumpkin Farm

Page 114
1. My pet Jilly
2. A helicopter ride

Page 124
1. 270, 420, 550, 700, 770, 920
2. 521, 522, 523, 524, 525, 526, 527, 528, 529
3. 275
4. 570
5. 520, 770, 920, 670

Page 115-124
From left to right :
1. 318, bedroom
2. 224, kitchen
3. 153, living room
4. 240, guest room
5. 165, bathroom
6. 419, family room
7. 361, dining room
8. 507, playroom

Page 126
Children will do on their own

Page 127
From left to right
194, 507, 132, 625, 314, 85

Page 128

Before		After
338	339	340
516	517	518
207	208	209
898	899	900
699	700	701

	Between	
399	400	401
628	629	630
147	148	149
512	513	514
765	766	767
771	772	773

Page 129
1. 30
2. 30
3. 60
4. 100
5. 700
6. 800
7. 500
8. 10
9. 5
10. 0
11. 900
12. 9
13. 300
14. 2
15. 600
16. 50
17. 400
18. 40

Page 130
Children will do on their own

Page 131
400 + 80 + 7
300 + 20 + 9
800 + 90 + 2
200 + 70 + 8
100 + 60 + 5
700 + 20 +3
700 + 30 + 5
800 + 10 + 8
600 + 90 + 5
200 + 20 + 4

Page 132
1. 469
2. 678
3. 954
4. 809
5. 514
6. 629
7. 180
8 . 754
9. 388
10. 581
11. 273
12. 455
13. 199
14. 704

Answer Key

Page 133

764 b. 536
818 d. 923
438 f. 839
503 h. 697

Page 135

1. 322 < 434
2. 444 < 515
3. 613 > 612

Page 134

om left to right
1, 809, 612
2, 891, 254 & 457
5, 218, 976
8, 786, 337

Page 136

1. No   2. Yes
3. No   4. No
5. Yes   6. Yes
7. No   8. Yes

Page 137

516, 561, 576   2. 324, 334, 343
260, 602, 620   4. 101, 113, 131
729, 734, 740   6. 800, 830, 893

Page 138

Six hundred and seventy nine
Three hundred and forty two
Nine hundred and eight
Five hundred and fifty six
Eight hundred and seventy six
Two hundred and fifty nine
Four hundred and forty five
One hundred and seventy eight
Seven hundred and eighty four
0. One hundred and nineteen

Page 139

a. 25 b.   35   c.   50
d. 5   e.   20   f.   45
g. 30 h.   15   i.   55
    40 k.   60   l.   10

numbers from least to greatest:
5, 10, 15, 20, 25, 30, 35, 40, 45,
50, 55, 60

Numbers from largest to smallest:
05, 115, 125, 135, 145, 155, 165,
175, 185, 195, 205, 215, 225, 235,
245, 255, 265, 275

Page 140

1. 110, 120   2. 330
3. 229, 235   4. 560, 575
5. 632, 634   6. 470, 480
7. 786, 788   8. 809, 812, 815,

RULE:

▭	Skip count by 10
●	Skip count by 5
▪	Skip count by 3
▲	Skip count by 2

Page 141

Children will do on their own

Page 142

2. 15   3. 5
4. 10   5. 40 minutes

Page 143

1. Children will do on their own
2. 80, 14, 15, 70
3. 344, 445, 355, 245

Page 144

1 and 2 children will do on their own
3. a. 244   b. 574, 585
   c. 548   d. 724, 728
   e. 485, 785

Page 146

Round 1: 10, 30, 10
Round 2: 20, 10, 20
Round 3: 10, 20, 30
Round 4: 10, 20, 20
Round 5: 20, 40, 30

Page 147

a. 600, 300
b. 900 ,600
c. 500, 900
d. 200, 600

Page 148

a. 34   b. 377   c. 83
d. 722   e. 48   f. 819
g. 56   h. 205   i. 346
j. 89

Page 150

1. 21st 2. 2
3. 4th floor   4. 13 floors
5. 21

Page 151

1. Gorilla, hippo, zebra, seal, giraffe
2. Zebra, giraffe, hippo, seal, gorilla
3. Hippo, elephant, giraffe, monkey
   gorilla
4. Fox, kangaroo, wolf, zebra, rhino

Page 152

Children will do on their own

Page 154

a. 17,   c. 12,   d. 20,   e. 20,
f. 16,   g. 12,   h. 20,   i. 12,
j. 14,   k. 16,   l. 10,   m. 13,
n. 10,   o. 10,   q. 15,   r. 9,
s. 12,   t. 11,   u. 16,   v. 17

Page 155

a. 29,   b. 59,   c. 89,   d. 45,
e. 59,   f. 67,   g. 77,   h. 63,
i. 97,   j. 98,   k. 78,   l. 78

Page 156

a. 82,   b. 102,   c. 121,   d. 42
Students to write expanded form on
their own.

Page 157

	1	8		5	6		1	8
3		7	6		4	9		6	7
1	6		3	9		3	5		2
	8	4			9		9		
6		3	7		2	4		2	5
9			5	9		1	7		7

Page 158

a. 101,   b. 84,   c. 62,   d. 65
e. 80,   f. 75,   g. 105,   h. 133
i. 81,   j. 61,   k. 104,   l. 130

Page 159

a. 638,   b. 585,   c. 579,   d. 927
e. 949,   f. 466,   g. 498,   h. 884
i. 889,   j. 988,   k. 847,   l. 489
The name of the cartoon is CHEEKY
MOUSE

Page 160

a. 1226,   b. 804,   c. 752,   d. 1401,
e. 681,   f. 1587,   g. 811,   h. 375,
i. 851,   j. 951

Page 161

a. 368,   b. 598,   c. 568,   d. 567,
e. 763,   f. 194,   g. 642,   h. 567,
i. 687,   j. 790,   k. 424,   l. 368,
m. 425,   n. 790

Answer Key

Page 162

$$58 + 42 = \underline{100} \text{ fruits}$$

$$640 + 310 = \underline{950} \text{ passengers}$$

$$356 + 274 = \underline{630} \text{ marbles}$$

Page 163

19 – 8 = 1 ___false___

5 – 0 = 0 ___false___

11 – 5 = 6 ___true___

10 – 2 = 8 ___true___

16 – 4 = 11 ___false___

14 – 4 = 10 ___true___

9 – 3 = 6 ___true___

17 – 9 = 6 ___false___

15 – 4 = 10 ___false___

18 – 9 = 9 ___true___

13 – 6 = 5 ___false___

11 – 5 = 6 ___true___

14 – 8 = 6 ___true___

17 – 7 = 10 ___true___

Page 164

a. 11,   b. 11,   c. 7,   d. 4,   e. 6,   f. 14,
g. 6,   h. 8,   i. 16,   j. 7,   k. 7,   l. 9,
m. 7,   n. 12,   o. 5,   p. 7,   q. 9,   r. 15,
s. 9,   t. 15

Challenge answer: number 2

Page 165

a. 15,   b. 14,   c. 41,   d. 20,   e. 25,   f. 19,
g. 21,   h. 42,   i. 61,   j. 50,   k. 82,   l. 60,

Page 166

a. 702,   b. 523,   c. 224,   d. 211,   e. 234,   f. 242,
g. 203,   h. 511,   i. 235,   j. 421

Page 167

T	O
6	3
– 3	4

T	O
⑤	¹³
6	̶3̶
– 3	4
2	9

T	O
⑦	¹³
̶6̶	̶3̶
– 3	4
2	9

1. Subtract the ___ones___ first.
   3 – 4 can't be done.
   You need to regroup

2. Borrow ___1___ ten from the
   ___tens___ .
   ___6___ – 1 = 5 in the tens
   column. 10 + ___3___ = 13
   in the ones column.

3. Now subtract. Ones first
   ___13___ – 4 = ___9___ Then the
   tens ___5___ – ___3___ = 2.

Page 168

a. 15,   b. 18,   c. 43,   d. 25,   e. 17,   f. 36,
g. 25,   h. 35,   i. 17,   j. 37,   k. 03,   l. 54,
m. 18,   n. 27,   o. 31

Page 169

1. Subtract the ___ones___ first.
   3 - 8 can't be done.
   Regroup 1 ten 4 ones as
   ___0___ tens and ___14___
   ones.

2. Subtract the tens ___0 – 8___
   can't be done.
   Borrow ___1___ hundreds
   from the ___hundreds___ column

3. Now subtract.
   Ones first ___14___ – 6 = ___8___
   Then the tens ___10___ – ___8___ = 2.
   At last the hundreds. ___8___ – ___4___ = ___4___

Page 170

a. 265,   b. 277,   c. 179,   d. 178   e. 389,   f. 429,
g. 88,   h. 355   i. 249,   j. 248,   k. 588,   l. 369
m. 189,   n. 519,   o. 178,   p. 168

Page 171

$$254 - 132 = \underline{122} \text{ cupcakes left}$$

$$224 - 75 = \underline{149} \text{ pages left}$$

$$425 - 127 = \underline{298} \text{ eggs left}$$

$$320 - 152 = \underline{168} \text{ yellow beads}$$

$$542 - 116 = \underline{426} \text{ passengers}$$

Page 172

Addition sums:

a. 15,   b. 20,   c. 15,   d. 15,   e. 16,   f. 22,
g. 22,   h. 21,   i. 21,   j. 25,   k. 17,   l. 26

Subtraction sums:

a. 6,   b. 10,   c. 13,   d. 8,   e. 8,   f. 6,
g. 3,   h. 9,   i. 13,   j. 9,   k. 5,   l. 11

Page 173

2	3	⑦
+ 4	①	8
6	5	5

7	⑦	7
– 2	8	⑤
④	9	2

⑥	7	7
+ 2	8	⑤
9	⑥	2

4	7	3
– ②	1	9
2	⑤	④

2	⑧	6
+ ⑤	1	9
8	0	5

5	0	6
– 2	9	①
2	①	5

4	7	3
+ ⑤	1	9
9	⑨	2

⑨	8	2
– 3	②	8
6	5	4

Answer Key

Page 174

$5 + 5 + 5 = 15$

$\boxed{5} \times \boxed{3} = \boxed{15}$

$+ 4 = \underline{\ 8\ }$

$3 + 3 + 3 + 3 + 3 = \underline{15}$

$\boxed{4} \times \boxed{2} = \boxed{8}$

$\boxed{3} \times \boxed{5} = \boxed{15}$

Page 175

2 × 2; b. 2 × 4;   c. 2 × 8; d. 3 × 5;   e. 3 × 6

Page 176

b) 4 × 8   2. a) 2 × 9   3. d) 6 × 7   4. c) 8 × 8

Page 177

× 6 = 18
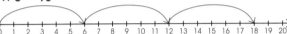

× 4 = 16

× 7 = 14
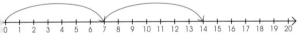

× 2 = 10

Page 178–181

Children will attempt on their own. Answers may vary.

Page 182

1 2 3 4	4 + 2 + 3 + 3
5 6 1 2	6 − 2 + 5 + 1 + 2
2 3 7 1	7 − 3 + 2 + 7 − 1
4 5 3 2	5 − 2 + 3 + 4 + 2

Page 184

3 – rectangle   4 – square
5 – hexagon   6 – triangle
7 – rectangle   8 – octagon
9 – square   10 – pentagon

Page 185

Rectangle   parallelogram

Square

Page 186

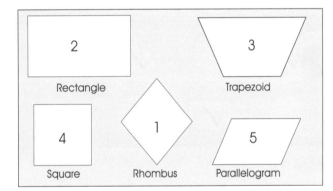

| 2 Rectangle | | 3 Trapezoid |
| 4 Square | 1 Rhombus | 5 Parallelogram |

Page 187

1.   a.   b.   c.

2.   a.   b.   c.

3.   a.   b.   c.

4.   a.   b.   c.

5.   a.   b.   c.

Answer Key

Page 188

1. E
2. O
3. A
4. NONE
5. I AND M
6. H
7. G
8. B
9. NONE
10. C
11. F
12. R

Page 189

Children will draw shapes on their own

Page 190

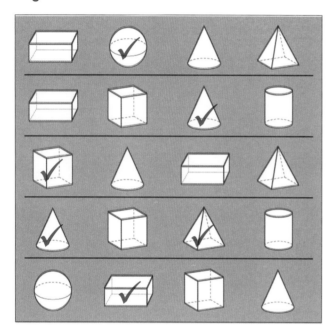

Page 191

Children will do on their own

Page 192

1. 6
2. 5 (write 2 under triangle and 3 under rectangle)
3. 6 (write 6 under square)
4. 6 (write 2 under square and 4 under rectangle)

Page 193

Children will do on their own

Page 194

1. Flip
2. Slide
3. Turn
4. Turn
5. Slide
6. Flip

Page 195

Children will do on their own

Page 196

Page 197

Answer Key

Page 199

1/2, 1/3, 1/4.
3, 6/9, 8/10, 7/9
5, 4/6, 4/7
12, 5/13, 10/14

Page 200

Children will do it on
their own

Page 201

30, 11:00, 1:00, 6:00
30, 8:00, 7:30, 11:30
30, 9:30, 2:00, 10:00

Page 202

:15, 2:15, 3:15, 4:15
:15, 6:15, 7:15, 8:15
:15, 10:15, 11:15, 12:15

Page 203

:15, 2:15, 3:15, 4:15
:15, 6:15, 7:15, 8:15
:15, 10:15, 11:15, 12:15

Page 204

Children will draw
hands on their own

Page 205

Children will do on their
own

Page 214

1. 9
2. Poppy, Emma, Pam
3. Poppy, Emma, Pam
4. Ronny
5. Apples and pears

Page 215

Pastime	Number of children
painting	4
reading	1
skating	3
cooking	3
playing football	2

Painting is most popular among Neo's friends.

Page 206

Children will do on their
own

Page 207

The length of paint
brush is 3 inches.
The length of the pencil
is 3 ¾ inches.

Page 208

3.5 kg, 750 g, 5.5 kg, 1.5 kg
3.8 kg, 2.3 kg, 750 g, 6.5 kg

Page 209

Children will do on
their own

Page 211

3 kg, 1kg
4 kg, 100g
50g, 3kg
5 kg, 100g

Page 211

1. 900 ml, 260 ml, 500 ml
2. 240 ml, 400 ml, 650 ml
3. Container A
4. 500 ml

Page 216

1. 20
2. 6
3. Social Science
4. Science
5. Writing

Page 217

Correct tally chart is:

Student	Tally count
Kate	ЖЖ ЖЖ ЖЖ ЖЖ ЖЖ ЖЖ II
Joy	ЖЖ ЖЖ ЖЖ ЖЖ III
Lilly	ЖЖ ЖЖ ЖЖ ЖЖ IIII
Suzie	ЖЖ ЖЖ ЖЖ ЖЖ ЖЖ II
Jill	ЖЖ ЖЖ ЖЖ

- We hope Kate to win the quiz.
- 5 things that we know from the tally chart:
1. Five students participated in the quiz.
2. Kate has scored the highest.
3. Jill has scored the lowest.
4. Suzie scored more than Joy.
5. Lily is 1 point ahead of Joy.

Page 219

Sea creature	Tally count
Turtle	ЖЖ II
Fish	ЖЖ ЖЖ
Starfish	ЖЖ III
Crab	ЖЖ IIII
Jelly Fish	III
Eel	ЖЖ II
Angelfish	ЖЖ I
Sea Horse	ЖЖ ЖЖ I
Shark	I

1. angelfish- 6   turtle - 7   shark - 1
   crab- 9   jelly fish- 3   starfish- 8
2. sea horse
3. 2
4. She saw 9 creatures to a count of 62

Answer Key

Page 220

1. Snow white and the Seven Dwarfs

2. Cinderella

3. Cinderella- 1000, Peter Pan- 1220, Beauty and the Beast- 1300, Rapunzel- 1560, Pinocchio- 2000,

4. Snow White and Seven Dwarfs- 2380

Page 221

1. France

2. Bangkok and France

3. Italy, Australia, Singapore

4. 18, 10, 9

Page 222

Piece of clothing	Frequency
Trousers	21
Shirt	10
Skirt	11
Shorts	19
Dress	15

1. Trousers- 21   Shirts- 10   Skirts- 11
Dresses- 15   Shorts-19

2. 3 for boys, 2 for girls

3. 76

4. By adding all the frequencies or tally counts

Page 223

Ants	●●●●
Caterpillars	●●●
Butterflies	●●●●
Bees	●●●●
Ladybirds	●●●●●●●●●
Beetles	●

ants- 4   caterpillars- 3   butterflies- 4   bees- 4
ladybirds- 9   beetles- 1

Page 225

Children will make the pictogram on their own.

How many of each instrument does
Mr Roger have?

violin- 8   drum -2   guitar-6   trumpet- 5   piano-

Page 226

Remote control car- 5   skates- 8   chocolates- 2   Board game- 10

water colours- 6   board game- 3

dress- 2   soft toy- 9   robot- 7

Page 227

Children will make pictogram on their own.

Page 228

Children will make pictogram on their own.

Page 230

1. dog- 7, cat- 9, fish- 3, guinea pig- 6, turtle- 5

2. cat

3. Fish

Page 231

1. Clown- 7, pirate- 3, sailor- 2,
   prince- 4, princess- 5, magician- 6

2. Clown

3. Sailor

Page 232

1. January- 7 degrees, April- 8 degrees, June- 15 degrees, August- 18 degrees, October- 14 degrees, December- 9 degrees

2. August

3. February

4. 18-6= 12 degrees

Page 233

1. Favourite snacks

2. Snack name

3. Numbers

4. Number of people

5. 0-15

Answer Key

Children will draw the bar chart on their own.

Subject	Number of books
Drawing	10
Physical Education	4
Painting	7
Creation	8
Geography	5
Maths	14
Geometry	11

Cookies	Number of boxes ordered
Orange Cookies	10
Choco chip cookies	8
Orange cookies	12
Strawberry cookies	9
Salty cookies	5
Oats cookies	6
Cashew cookies	15

Page 240
1. Strawberry-13, vanilla- 11, both- 3
   only strawberry- 10, only vanilla- 8
2. Ronny asked 18 friends.

Page 241
Children will make venn diagram on their own.

Answer Key

Page 245
Children will do on their own.

Page 248
Across: Down:

Across	Down
2 coat	1. parts
5. different	3. light
8. embryo	4. protects
10. sprout	6. food
12. eat	7. coconut
13. water	9. travel
14. wind	11. food

Page 249
True statements

Roots:	Stem:
1. Fix the plant in the soil. 2. Some roots like carrot, turnip, radish and beetroot store food in them.	1. Gives support to the plants. 2. Carries water and nutrients from the roots to the leaves. 3. Leaves, flowers, buds and fruits grow on the stem.
Leaves:	**Flowers:**
1. Help the plant breathe. 2. Store food.	1. Make seeds. 2. Attract insects and birds. 3. Store food.

Page 252

1. cotton
2. mint
3. coconut
4. watermelon
5. pea

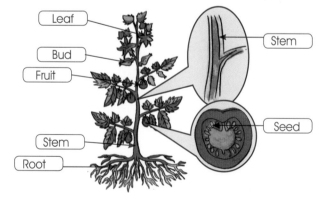

Page 252
Rose - thorns

Cactus - spikes

Touch me not plant - closes its leaves when touched

Lotus - waxy leaves to help it float on water

Poison ivy - produces an oil to protect itself

Page 255
Life cycle of butterfly:

Eggs, caterpillar, pupa, butterfly

Fill in the blanks:

1. leaf
2. larva
3. caterpillar
4. skin
5. two, butterfly

section 3:

sting and bite

colours and body

bad

Page 257
eggs, spiderlings, hatch, backs, spiderlings, spin, prey, autumn

Page 258
Reptiles:

chameleon, alligator, iguana, snake, crocodile, tortoise, lizard

True/false:

1. False
2. True
3. True
4. False
5. True

Page 259
Snakes:

- Have no legs
- Have a strong sense of smell
- Shed their skin
- Poison , fangs

Lizards:

- crawling
- bugs, insects, small creatures
- shedding their tail

Tortoises:

- shell
- land
- plants
- head and limbs

Answer Key

Page 260

egg

jelly

giills

legs

froglet

Page 261

feathers

wings

strong

boat shaped

beak

hollow, fly

Page 262

1. Long slender beak

2. Hooked beak

3. Slender curved beak

4. Spatulate beak

5. Small conical beak

6. Slender beak

7. Sharp beak

8. Short curved and downward-facing beak

9. Long slender beak

10. Spatulate beak

Page 263

1. elephant

2. dolphin

3. dog

4. bear

5. giraffe

Page 266

1. scales

2. protect

3. gills

4. membranes, breathe

5. steer, balance

6. tail

Page 267

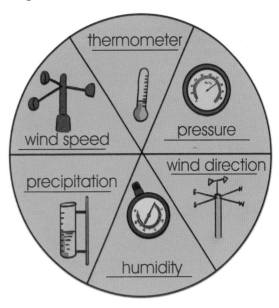

wind vane, thermometer, rain gauge

Page 268

temperature: hot, thermometer, hotter

wind: moving, warms, rises, cool, wind

humidity: moisture, oceans, heated, water vapour

air pressure: weight

Page 270

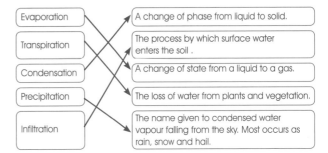

Answer Key

Page 274

play
celebrate festivals
read and study
go on a picnic

Page 275

1. False
2. True
3. True
4. True
5. True
6. True
7. True
8. true

Page 276

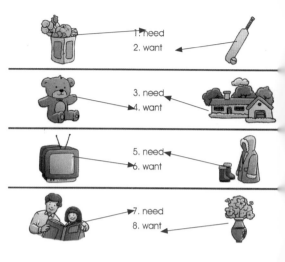

1. need
2. want
3. need
4. want
5. need
6. want
7. need
8. want

Page 277

1. cleaner's shop, grocery store,
   bus stop, hardware shop

2. Sterling Apartments

3. France Groceries

4. park

5. city

Page 279

Children will do on their own.
Answers will vary.

Answer Key

service

service

goods

goods

goods

service

Page 281

1. Library
2. Fire Department
3. Police
4. Park's Office
5. Ambulance
6. Post Office
7. Water Services
8. Garbage Collection
9. Animal Control
10. Power Company

Page 282

1. agree
2. agree
3. disagree
4. agree
5. disagree
6. agree
7. disagree
8. disagree
9. disagree
10. disagree

Page 283

1. The driver of the yellow car
2. The driver of the yellow car has skipped the red light.
3. The policeman should stop and warn him for breaking rules.

Page 284

Answer Key

Page 286

1. One
2. Read books
3. Newspaper
4. Sign board
5. Danger! No swimming

Page 287

1. Post office
2. E-mails
3. Telephone
4. Mobile phones
5. Television
6. Book
7. Newspaper

Page 288

1. False- Thousands of years ago, man used to travel from one place to another using carts, animals.
2. False- In rural areas, people usually travel by carts, other small vehicles.
3. False- Horses were used to pull carts some years ago
4. False- Things like coal, vehicles and goods are transported by goods trains.
5. False- The fastest means of transportation is aeroplane.
6. False- A submarine remains inside the water.
7. False- Trains run on steel tracks that are called tracks.
8. False- A helicopter can carry less number of people.

Page 290

Map A is Kate's neighbourhood

Page 291

1. Mom's room
2. Ron
3. Kim
4. Children will circle on their own
5. Seven

Page 292

1. North, south, east, west
2. North
3. East
4. South
5. West

Page 293

1. Monkey house
2. Tiger house
3. Elephant house
4. Two
5. Lion house would be to the left and no house on the right

Page 294

1. West
2. South
3. North
4. East

Page 295

1.

2. A house

3.

4. One

Page 296

1.

2.

3. five
4. Elm Street, Main Street, Oak Street, Maple Street
5. Children will circle the post office on their own

Page 297

1. Irish Sea, Celtic Sea
2. North
3. East
4. Children will draw symbols on their own
5. There are three rivers.

Page 299

1. Island
2. Lake
3. Plain
4. River
5. peninsula

Answer Key

age 300

ater, fruits, soil, wool and wood
e natural resources

age 301

hese are ways to take care of
atural resources:

Throw litter in the trash can

Use things again

Take care of birds and animals

Help to keep the surroundings
clean

Answer Key